A
SWING
YOU CAN
TRUST

A
SWING
YOU CAN
TRUST

A Breakthrough Approach for Confident, Low-Scoring Play

Roberto Borgatti

ATRIA BOOKS

New York London Toronto Sydney

ATRIA BOOKS

A Division of Simon & Schuster, Inc.
1230 Avenue of the Americas
New York, NY 10020

First Atria Books hardcover edition June 2007

ATRIA BOOKS and colophon are trademarks of Simon & Schuster, Inc.

For information regarding special discounts for bulk purchases, please contact
Simon & Schuster Special Sales at 1-800-456-6798 or business@simonandschuster.com.

Designed by Joel Avirom and Jason Snyder

Manufactured in the United States of America

10   9   8   7   6   5   4   3   2   1

Library of Congress Cataloging-in-Publication Data

Borgatti, Roberto.
  A swing you can trust : a breakthrough approach for confident, low-scoring
play / Roberto Borgatti.
     p. cm.
  1. Golf—Study and teaching. I. Title.
  GV962.5.B67 2007
  796.352'3—dc22   2006038643

ISBN-13: 978-0-7432-9828-5
ISBN-10:   0-7432-9828-4

FOR MY UNCLE JIM

CONTENTS

PART I
THE FULL SWING: FOUR STEPS
TO A PHENOMENAL GOLF SWING

PART II
THE SHORT GAME: WHERE ART MEETS SCIENCE

PART III
SPECIAL SHOTS AND DRILLS

PART IV
PRACTICE FOR YOUR BEST GOLF

FOREWORD

by Ian Baker Finch

A WELL-KNOWN GOLF ANNOUNCER once said you can't learn to play golf from a book. The fact that you are reading this means you disagree. I do, too, and I'll tell you why.

I grew up on a farm in Queensland, Australia, in the 1960s, and my father, Tony, caught the golfing bug by watching "the big three" winning the Majors. Dad and some friends decided a local golf course was needed, and they built one—the Beerwah Golf Club. It opened in 1971 and I was eleven years old. I started to caddy for my dad, and caught the bug myself. Dad gave me my first set of clubs on my twelfth birthday. I won the State Schoolboy Title at thirteen, and again at fifteen. A year later I turned pro and completed a three-year PGA trainee program before joining the World tours.

My coach through the early years was not my dad. It was Jack Nicklaus—or more accurately, *Golf My Way*, written by Jack Nicklaus. I read it from cover to cover and modeled my game on what Jack told me in that book. *Golf My Way* became my golfing bible. I still have it and enjoy referring to it, as I'm sure many other golfers—professionals and weekenders—have done for many years. Thanks to instructional books, thousands of golfers enjoy better games every day.

Roberto Borgatti is no Jack Nicklaus, and that's where his strength lies as an author and as an instructor. In *A Swing You Can Trust*, Roberto's not writing about his own game, but about *your* game. His book provides a complete package—a clearly explained and illustrated step-by-step process to better golf that everyone can relate to, be they novice or 5-handicapper. The fundamentals are here, for sure, but the book also outlines innovative swing training and exercise techniques, and shows you new ways to accomplish the most difficult shots facing you on the course.

Thanks to its focus on swing fundamentals that can be easily applied to any swing, you'll find that *A Swing You Can Trust* will be *your* golfing bible; it will keep you coming back for more. I know I'll keep a copy handy. With the help of Roberto's swing training and techniques, I hope to have my game back in shape for the Champion's Tour.

PREFACE

by Patrick Lencioni
author of *The Five Dysfunctions of a Team*

SOMETIMES THE TITLE OF A BOOK says it all. This is one of those books.

For too many of us, this wonderful sport called golf becomes a game of frustration. Whether we play professionally on a tour, competitively at our local country club, or socially with friends and business colleagues, we can all relate to that moment when we're out on the course asking ourselves the big question: "Why? Why do I keep subjecting myself to this disappointment and frustration?"

And then we hit a nice shot and we ask ourselves a different question, one that is at the heart of this book: "Why? Why don't I do that every time? Starting on the next hole, I'm going to do it that way again." And then we don't, and we go back to the first question.

This is where it is critical to take a long, hard look at the source of our disappointment.

If you're anything like me, your greatest frustration with golf doesn't come from misreading a putt or choosing the wrong club for an approach shot or misjudging the wind. Those variables—undulations on a green, pin placements, changing weather—are what make golf a great game.

If I wanted every course to be the same, and every putt to roll perfectly straight, then I'd be playing croquet or billiards.

The real source of my frustration with golf is embodied in that moment when I read the putt correctly or judge the distance and the wind accurately, and then fail to hit the ball the way my mind tells my body to hit it. I get angry not because my score is going to be adversely affected, but because I feel that I have let myself down. My body has somehow betrayed my mind. It is as though a civil war is raging inside me, and what makes matters worse, I don't understand why.

Roberto Borgatti's book has changed all that. His method has restored my passion for a game that I love to watch, talk about, and play. What makes Roberto's method so powerful is its comprehensive simplicity. Rather than clouding my game with micro-suggestions about club speed or selection, he taught me how to go back to the basics of what a golf swing is.

In doing so, Roberto gave me something much more valuable than the ability to hit the ball straighter and much farther than I could before—though that was certainly nice. He saved my game just as I was about to throw my clubs into the proverbial lake. Before I could abandon my hopes for teaching my kids to golf, he taught me that it is possible to trust myself, my ability, my swing. And that is all I really wanted.

After all, I am content to let the greenskeeper or the weather or the time of day have its way with me. They are worthy adversaries. I just don't want to be my own worst enemy.

INTRODUCTION

Discover the Joy of Playing Golf

IF GOLFERS COULD BE GRANTED ONE WISH, aside from a full membership at Augusta National, it would likely be a swing they could trust. An overwhelming barrage of information confronts the player seeking a clear and simple understanding of the swing. It's my goal to help you achieve this—a swing both powerful and effective, along with the ability to score.

Golfers are made, not born. Like good manners, proper golf form is learned. Many principles of good form are counterintuitive, so following one's natural inclinations or instincts does not guarantee success. Great athletes are not necessarily great golfers. Coordination and strength complement proper technique, but alone, they are insufficient.

This book is a system of learning, not a compendium of tips. Golf tips are as useful in improving your technique as painkillers are in treating disease. They may provide temporary relief by taking your mind off conscious efforts at hitting, controlling, and steering the ball so you can swing more freely, but they rarely solve the underlying problem. So that's not real progress. A day or two later, you're no better off. *This book will allow you to identify what is essential and how to achieve a powerful and reliable golf swing.*

I have helped golfers move their scores from 100 to the 80s and 70s, and helped top amateurs and pros to win tournaments. Whether you are an amateur or a professional, the same principles apply. Many golfers lack only the proper training and development program to maximize their potential.

When using this book, first, you'll find an explanation of each concept, followed by an exercise or drill. In many chapters, a "Taking It on the Golf Course" section helps you incorporate that element while playing. Chapter 10, "Drills for Skill Development," features actual players I coach.

This book could have been named *A Golf Game You Can Trust,* as it covers all the aspects of the game you will need to understand to become an accomplished player. Besides golf drills focused on technique, you'll find a golf-specific fitness section designed to improve your strength, flexibility, and coordination.

My system is a complete course for both beginners learning the game and experienced golfers seeking to perfect and refine their skill. Even if you have limited time, it offers all the opportunity to discover and experience that "game-turning moment." While you may be tempted to turn to a section where you most need help, I recommend you first scan the entire work as presented, in order for you to see its logical and natural progression.

I hope this book will make your golf journey an enjoyable one. However technical or demanding, playing better golf is ultimately a labor of love. Nothing is accomplished without making a commitment, so do that now—and start building a swing you can trust.

Part I

The Full Swing

Four Steps to a Phenomenal Golf Swing

TO DEVELOP A GREAT GOLF SWING, you need to master four fundamentals, which I refer to as the core four. Plain and simple, their execution equates to performance.

What's new and different in my approach is the attention I pay to several critical factors in each of the four fundamentals. Each of these factors is counterintuitive, which may explain why they often go unrecognized or neglected. But once you understand them, you'll be able to begin making the same sorts of breakthroughs in your game that I see regularly with the students and professionals I teach.

MASTERY OF THE CORE FOUR

In this section, I'll take you through the core four:

- Swing motion

- Setup

- Turn

- Weight shift

These four interdependent elements *are* your swing. When properly executed and coordinated, they cause hundreds of successive movements to occur fluidly, without conscious effort.

I will explain why each of these moves is important and how to execute it. In each case, I'll emphasize a neglected key factor that can unlock the power of your swing. I'll give you a set of exercises and drills to turn understanding into performance. The overwhelming point on mastering technique is that when you are playing, you actually shouldn't be thinking about it; it should be the farthest thing from your mind.

You will be surprised how quickly and intuitively your body will respond.

1
SWING MOTION

"**HOW DID YOU HIT** the ball today?"

That's one of the most common questions you'll hear golfers ask one another after a day of play. But it's also one of the most misguided for anybody who wants to execute a great swing.

In baseball or tennis, where the ball is moving—often very fast—your object *is* to "hit the ball." In both of these sports there's a lot of emphasis on proper hand-eye coordination.

But in golf, where the ball is stationary, trying to "hit the ball" is the underlying cause of many a faulty golf swing. In golf, your object should be to move your club and body through space in a consistent, repeatable way. If you can learn to do that while holding a club, you'll be able to move a golf ball around the course with power and precision.

But it all starts with swing motion—with how your body moves through space, even when you are not holding a club. It's much more like dancing than like baseball or tennis, which explains one of the joys of mastering golf. It's a sport that really involves your entire body in a coordinated effort, combining grace and power.

The key factor for a correct swing is developing a feel for how your *entire body moves from the beginning, through an intermediate point, to the end of the swing.*

It is a common misconception that the golf swing is largely about *hand-eye coordination.* This was made clear to me while working at the 2004 World Golf Championships, where I met with Guy Delacave, director of the European Tour Van, a traveling physiotherapeutic center on wheels that makes all the tour stops. Guy explained, "It is proprioception"—the physical awareness of motion through space without seeing—"that is more important than hand-to-eye coordination." While one of his staff continued to massage Luke Donald, who mustered a nod while lying prone, Guy demonstrated this by closing his eyes and trying to touch his fingers behind his back. It was that ability, innate or acquired, to move through space and return to exactly the same place, that is required in the swing.

Of course all those pieces are involved, and indeed lots of golf instruction teaches you how to move one of them separately, then another, then another. But the piecemeal approach actually works against what you ultimately must learn and feel: having all the parts working effortlessly together. I've found that it's actually easier for students to get all their body parts moving together right from the start than to learn how to integrate them later.

To develop that feel, try the Swing Motion drill:

1. Stand tall.

2. Simply turn your body and shift your weight.

3. Next, bend forward from the hips into more of a golf posture, and make the same motion.

4. Finally, repeat the same motion with a golf club and ball.

THE SWING MOTION DRILL

Standing up straight, extend your arms in front of you. Turn your body and shift your weight.

Next, bend over from the hips, into a golf posture, and make the same motion.

Finally, do the same with a golf club and ball. Don't try to hit the ball. Focus on the swing.

You may be surprised how natural and graceful your swing suddenly feels! Especially at the onset, the simple act of feeling the general Swing Motion is the singularly most important element, the cornerstone of your development.

As time passes, you will share my conviction that the Swing Motion is the "lifeblood" of your swing. Its benefits include:

- **A clear perspective.** Knowing how your body moves and "swings the club" puts you way ahead of those trying to "hit the ball." You are seeing the big picture before focusing on any individual element. Even if you are an experienced player, this powerful exercise can help you override an inefficient swing motion.

- **A conditioned move.** Your top priority is developing a conditioned and consistent movement that takes the club through space. When you've repeated this exercise a few hundred times, as your muscle memory increases, your swing will begin to assume its ideal shape.

    You may also try this exercise with your eyes closed. When you eliminate the visual component, you experience a heightened physical sensation and further develop your "proprioceptive" abilities.

- **Power.** The Swing Motion exercise engages the larger, stronger core muscles, thereby generating the most powerful and efficient motion. Athletic posture, pivot, and rotation become the blueprint for all powerful athletic motions. By learning these positions, you will automatically rotate your body and shift your weight. Rotation and weight shift underlie the biomechanics of many sports, including tennis, skiing, baseball, and basketball.

I recently brought this point up with Jay Feely, place kicker for the New York Giants, and perhaps the best golfer in the NFL (a scratch player "in season"). He told me emphatically that the mechanics of his golf swing and kicking motion have fundamental similarities. As you progress through this book, you may start to recognize this truth and apply what you have learned in other sports you play.

YOUR UNIQUE SWING

How should my swing look? Should I model it after the swing of a tour pro whose physique is similar to mine?

The look of your swing will be determined by your individual physical traits: your body's geometry, proportions, flexibility, and muscularity. Each person has an individual swing. Thus each person has his or her unique swing look. What you want to develop is an *effective* swing, not a swing look.

The Swing Motion exercise builds your individual swing without forcing you into a mold. It allows for the natural variation across bodies, since no two people are exactly alike. It requires the right mechanics, but is not a straitjacket. Allow your unique swing to take shape within the framework of sound fundamentals. While a particular tour professional's swing may appeal to you aesthetically, it may relate only remotely to your physicality.

In Clifford Odets's play *Awake and Sing,* the character Jake, a barber, has the right idea. Complimented on his craft, he responds, "Not one haircut for all . . . I make the haircut to fit the face."

Likewise, your unique swing will reflect your individuality.

Taking It on the Golf Course: Trusting the Swing

Whether you are a beginner facing your first round or an improving experienced golfer, you should always visualize the motion and keep it in the forefront of your mind. When playing, it is easy to get nervous and go back to your comfort zone, even if it means returning to bad habits. Once the ball and target is before you, you will be inclined to "direct the ball" instead of trusting your new, repeatable full-bodied swing. You must learn to distinguish between conscious execution (directing the ball) and involuntary response (trusting your body). Building that trust is a day-to-day process.

A trick that seems to work very well, particularly for those blessed with a vivid imagination, is to invert reality. On your practice swing, imagine the ball *is actually there.* On your actual swing, imagine the ball is not there and just swing through as you did on your practice swing.

Andrew Arkin, a golf student of mine turned friend and mentor in life, put this idea in beautiful perspective. After a morning's tuition on the practice range, we were ready to tee off on the first hole at Fenway Golf Club in Scarsdale, New York, when he leaned over and said quietly, "Roberto, the number for today is twenty-five." "Twenty-five?" I asked him. "That's right—*twenty-five good swings.* I'm playing for *swing* today, not *score*!"

On the fifteenth hole, Andrew hit a brilliant shot from an impossibly deep bunker that hit the pin and stopped inches from the hole. Not hesitating, he said, "Well, I reached my quota." By the time we holed out on the eighteenth, Andrew had surpassed his quota by five.

I suggest you try this so that soon your actual swings will be as good as or better than your practice swings!

2
SETUP

PROPER SETUP—WHICH INCLUDES POSTURE, GRIP, aim, and ball position—is a vital precondition for a good swing. A bad setup takes as much away from your game as poor swing mechanics or fatigue. You simply can't strike the ball consistently well unless you start from the right position, one that represents your most natural alignment and provides a solid foundation. From the right setup you should feel balanced and athletic, more ready than rigid.

POSTURE

Standing Tall

Setup begins with proper posture. It will help you avoid many swing faults. The most celebrated golf instructors and elite sports trainers emphasize the importance of the body's alignment in all movement sequences. Your body's alignment and movement efficiency are intertwined.

Maximum clubhead speed and *efficiency of movement* are generated from a starting position that reflects the body's most natural alignment, balance, and leverage capabilities. When you stand tall, like a soldier at attention or a dancer, your spinal column is lined up, with one vertebra on top of the other, rather than twisted and compressed. This allows you to make a beautiful, unencumbered rotation. The only difference between standing tall and your golf posture is the change of spinal angle. A powerful swing requires this pure posture. We can all achieve this.

Unfortunately, faults in posture can easily go unrecognized or misdiagnosed. Correct posture involves not one but two tilts of your spine. Most golf instruction emphasizes the first and ignores or glosses over the crucial second tilt. Failure to achieve proper posture will put an immediate ceiling on your potential as a player.

> **See chapter 12 of this book for exercises to increase your body's overall strength, stability, and natural alignment, all the elements that influence your posture.**

Primary Tilt

The first tilt—the one we all know—is the tilt toward the ball. Pretend you're standing at attention. While maintaining the integrity of your spinal column (chest high, stomach drawn in, and buttocks tucked under), simply bend from the hips. Joel Fedder, one of my more erudite students, practices doing this in front of a mirror.

You want your spinal column to be aligned and each muscle in its most natural lengthened state, so all your muscles are available to work together in a powerful motion. No muscles in and around the shoulders should be compressed or unnaturally stretched. This ultimately results in your achieving maximum efficiency and power.

On the facing page, you will find an approach I've found very effective in helping my students align their bodies correctly and move into the primary tilt with their weight properly balanced.

1

Stand tall with the club in your left hand. Minimize the curve in your back by tucking in your stomach and buttocks so that your shoulders and hips line up.

2

Bend over from the hip joint, balancing on the ball of your front foot, and let your arms hang down and grip the club normally.

3

Bring your foot back to the ground, and assume your setup position.

At the onset, you may feel unfamiliar tensions in isolated places in your body. Eventually, you will achieve a natural alignment without increasing tension. More important, as you do this exercise more and more, you will not need someone else's critique of your posture, because you are going to feel the difference between right and wrong.

Secondary Tilt

Golf instruction often stops with the primary tilt. As better instructors will tell you, you don't have proper posture without a secondary tilt of the spine away from the target. It's a movement that seems counter to our natural inclination toward and appreciation for symmetry. But it's necessary to adjust for the fact that one hand is lower than the other on the club. How you make that small adjustment has tremendous impact on the rest of your game.

Tragically, most amateurs drop their right shoulder, twisting and compressing their spinal vertebrae and compromising their core muscles. Instead, initiate the movement from the hips while maintaining the feeling of an elongated spine, thereby preserving your alignment. Your hips should shift slightly forward toward the target as you adopt this secondary tilt. Your left hip should be slightly higher than your right. This is what all the world's best players do to achieve the unfettered rotation of shoulders and torso that gives them such tremendous power.

The secondary tilt is not a "natural" motion for most people. I cannot remember one case in which a beginner naturally assumed the correct posture by instinct. You have to work to develop it. But if you do not include this secondary tilt, you will invariably compromise your spinal integrity.

The correct way to lower the right hand is by a second tilt of the spine away from the target.

YES

NO

Bend and tilt from the hips!

Only dropping the right shoulder.

GRIP

Holding the club in a manner that maximizes stability and leverage must be Priority No. 1. With the proper grip, the golf club will sit stably in your hands with minimum effort or pressure. A tense, tight grip will impede proper hand movement through the swing. Hold the club "as if you had a small bird in your hand," as Sam Snead was fond of saying.

Take the "ultimate grip test." Place the club in your left hand so the butt end tucks under the pad of your hand (see left photo below). Now release your three trail fingers. If the club remains in place, your grip is correct. The heel, or pad, of your hand supports the weight of the club, allowing your middle, ring, and pinkie fingers to relax. The club is held stable on this "plane," balanced nicely underneath the heel pad and left forefinger.

Hold the club as shown so that the pad of your hand is on top of the club and the forefinger underneath.

Let go with the last three fingers. If your grip is correct, the club will remain balanced in place.

When the hands ultimately come together, the forefinger of your left hand and the pinkie finger on your right interlock or overlap, as depicted. Whether you decide to overlap or interlock your hands is entirely up to you. You will find that interlocking may be more comfortable if you have small hands. This connection helps left and right hands work together in a more unified fashion than simply placing them side by side in baseball fashion (referred to as a ten-finger grip).

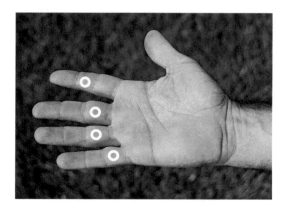

Club should lie on 2nd and 3rd metacarpals (highlighted).

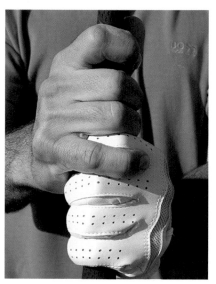

AIM

Aiming at a target seems too simple a concept to merit a section of its own. Any experienced golfer, however, will admit just how challenging perfect aim is. The world's best players never take it for granted.

Why such a challenge? The simple reason is vantage point. Our binocular vision naturally wants to look straight down the target line, which is why golfers are well advised to stand behind the ball when lining up the shot. But once we move to address, the aim we had locked in only a moment before is often lost, because standing alongside the ball makes it difficult to judge what is truly on line. In the absence of a couple of guiding principles, a majority of right-handed golfers will aim to the right of their intended target—yet they will think they are lined up perfectly.

"X" MARKS THE SPOT

"Railroad tracks"—the clubface points at the target (referred to as the "target line"), while your stance, hips, and shoulders are set parallel to this line.

With this kind of setup, the ball will naturally start to the right of your target. The golfer then attempts to compensate by swinging across the line—grooving a most imperfect swing, of the slice-producing variety.

Your objective: to aim the clubface at the target, your body (stance, hips, and shoulders) aligned "parallel left." To achieve dead aim, as shown in the photo sequence on the following page, begin by standing *behind* the ball to find the appropriate line to the target. Then choose a spot on the ground a few yards ahead of the ball that is on this line. This technique was popularized by Jack Nicklaus and is an essential ingredient to proper aim. Look for something that will still be identifiable when you move to the address position—a distinctive leaf, twig, pebble, divot, tuft of crabgrass, or any other object.

When you address the ball, aim the clubface at this intermediate target and set your feet parallel to an imaginary line drawn between it and the ball. If you are lined up correctly, your stance and shoulders will feel as if they are aimed at a spot parallel to but slightly left of your ultimate target.

BALL POSITION

Compare the driver, 6 iron, and wedge in the photos on page 21. The distance you stand from the ball varies with the length of each club—farthest away for the driver and closest for the wedge. Do not stand "taller" with the longer clubs to draw the ball closer to you. As you see in frame B, your spine angle should remain relatively consistent no matter which club you are swinging. This allows you to make virtually the "same swing" with all your clubs.

1
Pick your target.

2
Aim clubface at an intermediate point in line with your target.

3
Take your stance (feet, hips, and shoulders) parallel to the target line.

Forward or Back in the Stance?

In frame A, note how the *driver is placed forward in the stance.* This position encourages a level or even slightly upward strike. Meanwhile, the irons are placed progressively farther back to ensure a downward strike—contact with the ground should occur *after* striking the ball.

Rather than change your swing for each club, you must simply identify and respect its natural arc and let it determine placement of the ball. Consciously attempting to hit down on the ball can produce wild outcomes due to inevitable inconsistency in your club's path to the ball.

In frame A, note how the shaft of the driver is vertical, while the shafts of the *irons lean forward,* toward your target. This forward lean helps encourage a more downward blow, which compresses the ball against the clubface and the ground, producing backspin.

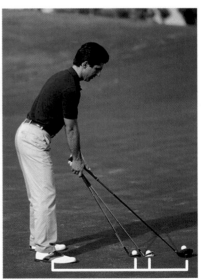

A
*Hand position is consistent—
ball position varies.*

B
*Spine angle is consistent—
distance from ball varies.*

ARMS AND HANDS

Arms' Distance from the Body

There is a common misconception that the arms should hang straight down at address. In most cases this is too close to your torso and will cramp your swing. When you're making a full swing, centrifugal force naturally sends your arms away from your body. As shown below, my hands at the point of impact are under my chin, not my shoulders. My arms have migrated some two or three inches away from their natural "hanging" position. This position should be adopted at address.

The distance of your arms at address varies with the individual and is determined largely by your body geometry. The best way to estimate *where your arms should be at address* is to identify where they will go naturally when you make your swing. Otherwise you will be forced to make

At the moment of impact, centrifugal force sends the arms slightly away from the body.

compensations in either your spine angle or your swing plane to achieve clean contact. This sounds complicated, but fortunately it is easy to solve with the following exercise:

SWING AND STOP EXERCISE

To find where to set your arms: Make a normal swing but stop at impact.

- **Set up without a ball.**

- **Take your swing, without guiding the club but letting the Swing Motion happen.**

- **Now, do it again, but STOP just before impact. Notice the position of your arms.** *That's where they should be at address!*

1

Make your normal backswing.

2

Stop yourself at impact.

Hand Position

Your hands should always meet where your left arm hangs naturally. Typically this is opposite the inside of your left thigh and mirrors the correct impact position, where the club shaft and the left arm form a straight line. Quite often inexperienced players make the mistake of setting their hands too far back, resulting in a sharp angle between the left arm and the club shaft. This introduces an extra variable because the shaft has to move at some point during the upswing from this "middle" position to being in line with the forward arm in order to achieve proper impact. Instead, allow your left arm and your irons to form a straight line, the same position you will return to at impact. The exception is your driver; because of its forward ball position, allow for a slight angle between your left arm and the club.

Ball Position

One of golf's luxuries is that you strike the ball when it is at rest. Where to stand and when to strike is entirely up to you, but it is essential to establish a standard placement, one we can count on. Playing the ball opposite the inside of your left heel with your driver, and in between that point and the middle of your stance with your irons, is a generic starting point for everyone. Since the bottom of the swing arc lies approximately underneath the left armpit, this results in the ball being struck ever so slightly on the rise with your driver and ever so slightly descending with your irons. As you improve, the bottom of your swing arc may change, moving forward. Beginners may benefit by playing the irons in the middle of the stance, but this should be no more than a transitional stage. While it may help them achieve a downward blow, it develops, if not monitored, into a reluctance to shift to the front foot. If you are heavyset, I recommend adopting a standard stance width, from which you change ball position from iron to iron.

3

TURN

ROTATING YOUR BODY CORRECTLY is one of the basic skills you need to master to create an effective, powerful swing. A good turn is as essential to the swing as the air you breathe. In the golf swing, the body rotates, or *turns* around an axis—the spine. Many drills and instructional aids have been devised throughout golf history to instill a "proper turn." They often fall short of achieving the ideal—a smooth, efficient release of muscular energy in a way that unites all of your musculature, maximizes leverage, and is repeatable.

When your shoulders turn in this manner, all the larger muscles of the torso (lats, abs, and deltoids) work in unison to generate maximum clubhead speed. Furthermore, turning your shoulders and torso on the same plane allows you the largest degree of unfettered rotation. This motion is far healthier and puts less stress on the back; nevertheless, it is not most individuals' natural inclination from the golf posture.

THE KEY TO POWER: TURNING YOUR SHOULDERS PERPENDICULAR TO YOUR SPINE

Most people, if asked to strike a punching bag, will instinctively turn their shoulders into the punch in a way that usually comes close to maximizing their leverage. Even if they have never taken a boxing class, their natural instinct generates a powerful motion, similar to one that can be applied to the golf swing.

The challenge starts as soon as you address the ball. From the traditional golf posture, you lack a definitive point of reference to determine the exact angle of your rotation: whether or not your shoulders are in fact turning correctly (perpendicularly). In fact, it is an absurd waste of energy to figure it out from there. Fortunately, there is a remedy.

HOW TO MAKE THE CORRECT TURN

You can quickly teach yourself the correct "perpendicular" turn. The turn exercise will eliminate any ambiguity concerning this potentially enigmatic motion. It produces an immediate effect and irrefutable evidence that you are turning properly. You can watch yourself in a mirror to make sure your movement is correct.

1. Start by standing at attention. Your spinal column forms a vertical line, your shoulders a horizontal one.

2. Grip your club normally in your left hand and underneath with the right, hands shoulder width apart, and hold them straight out in front of you so they are even with your shoulders (at shoulder height). Turn your shoulders level to the ground (horizontally), rotating on the desired path.

3. Now complete the motion in the reverse direction. If your shoulders are still level, you have achieved a correct turn and can begin building the desired muscle memory.

An easy turn, 1, 2, 3 . . .

When you stand erect, your spine forms an essentially vertical line (highlighted in white), while your shoulders form a horizontal one. Turn your shoulders so they remain level, moving perpendicularly to the spine. After you have done this a couple of times, bend over into your golf posture without wasting a moment, and try to feel the same rotation. I emphasize immediately, because, as Gravity Golf guru David Lee likes to point out, muscle memory lasts only about three seconds.

After only brief repetition, this will begin to feel natural. The feeling, once internalized, will rarely abandon you. Whenever it does, you have this exercise, no pun intended, to turn to. I recommend you make this exercise part of your warm-up and practice routine in order to continually refine your turn.

Left to his or her own devices, the struggling enthusiast tends to turn the shoulders on a path that teachers generally label as "steep," putting the onus on arms and shoulders, greatly compromising potential energy. Such motion is commonplace because the natural inclination is to direct the club along the target line, drawing your shoulders along this overly "steep" path and down the wrong road.

This errant motion, besides being generally ineffective and power-sapping, can cause a number of commonly diagnosed swing faults—reverse pivot, closed clubface, and improper hand action.

TURN . . . UNTIL WHEN?

A 90-degree shoulder turn seems to be everyone's ideal, and it is a pretty good benchmark. Your body type and flexibility will largely determine how far your shoulders can turn. Nevertheless, you can aim for the biggest turn possible, as long as you maintain your balance and posture. Once you reach the limit of your natural shoulder rotation, stop. Never push or force the turn. Otherwise you will likely lose important angles in your body.

Taking It on the Golf Course: The Ultra-Important First Inch

The correct rotation of the shoulders must begin at the very first instance of movement. The common tendency is to immediately drop the forward shoulder or draw it directly back. Instead, *this crucial first movement of the left shoulder should be forward (as indicated by the arrow in the middle frame, opposite), staying level,* and not straight back or down. Hence, the path of the left shoulder should be toward the ball, then under your chin. You should guard against the natural inclination to drop the left shoulder or immediately pull it straight back, both of which will result in too steep a swing. Should this way of turning feel unfamiliar, it will no doubt eventually come more naturally. Just stay with it, and in a very short time you may likely need to account for an extra ten or fifteen yards.

STAYING ON THE LEVEL

Left shoulder moves forward toward the ball, then back! The correct tracking of the left shoulder is an initial move forward. As shown clearly in the third frame, the left shoulder makes its way under the chin after this initial movement forward.

4
WEIGHT SHIFT

"SHIFT YOUR WEIGHT": The phrase is so simple and so often uttered, yet so easily misunderstood.

Golf instruction often directs you to "load the right side," and in the next breath tells you to "stay centered" or "don't sway." Such contradictory advice has probably left you confused, impossibly trying to make a centered rotation while shifting your weight.

The confusion is largely one of terminology and translation. Most golfers think of "weight shift" as a movement from your right foot to your left foot. While this may be a correct sensation, it is not the underlying action of the effective shift. Inevitably it leads to an exaggerated shift in the lower body—a swing fault called a "sway." A shift of this sort is counterproductive and destabilizes the swing.

Managing your weight shift properly has a profound impact on the swing. The essential key is that a subtle *weight shift should occur primarily from the waist up. It is your upper body that moves, shifting the center of gravity.* Johnny Miller refers to "a swing within the swing." The sensation in the lower body should be one of "loading," remaining stable by absorbing or "resisting" the shift of the center of gravity to your back foot. This resistance is important for generating more power and fostering precise contact. When done properly, it will give you the feeling of being "grounded."

Instead of the lower body being the principal actor, the upper body is actually the source of the weight shift. Meanwhile *the sensation is felt in the lower body*—a solid base for the movement. Properly executed, this shift produces two tangible benefits, advancing our quest for power and repeatability.

HOW TO MAKE THE SHIFT

The motion demonstrations on the following page represent two swing possibilities. One is correct, the spine highlighted white. One is incorrect, the spine highlighted white to red.

In exhibit A, correct lateral motion of the upper body is shown—the entire body above your waist shifts ever so slightly. Note the constancy of the right leg, an immovable post of resistance and stability. Exhibit B shows a common tendency—the head remains fixed, causing the lower part of the spine and the hips to shift or sway.

The desired sensation: When you are doing it correctly, here's what will happen—and you won't even have to think about it! As your center of gravity shifts, you still want to feel that you maintain stable contact with the ground in both feet. You should feel a little more pressure on the right going back, and on the left to initiate the start of the downswing. Note how at the top of the backswing (exhibit A, figure at right), there is little or no breakdown of the right leg, which stays slightly flexed and angled toward the target.

To achieve a proper weight shift, you must center your weight over the balls of your feet. As shown in the photo sequence on page 36, centering the weight helps create resistance and promotes proper mechanics, particularly at the top of the swing.

A CORRECT LATERAL SHIFT

A

Better biomechanics: Allow your head and upper body to shift (above), so that your lower body doesn't, as in the images below.

THE MOST COMMON ERROR

B

Head and upper body stay fixed, inhibiting correct movement and causing lower body to shift or sway.

NO: NEVER ON THE HEELS!

*Hips overrotate and right leg straightens, leading
to a loss of resistance and balance.*

YES: BALLS OF THE FEET!

*With weight moving along the balls of the feet,
knee flex remains constant in frame 2.*

Balance and Resistance Unite. If your weight is on your toes or heels, you will have a hard time maintaining your equilibrium. Instead, keep your weight on the balls of your feet as your center of gravity shifts. This will benefit your swing by . . .

1. Restricting your hip turn, producing torque.

2. Facilitating an easy transition from backswing to downswing.

The degree to which your center of gravity moves depends on your individual anatomy (your body's proportions, dimensions, and flexibility) and the width of your stance.

Leading sports scientist Dr. Laurence Holt weighs in on the subject: "The timing, the amount of the unweighting, and the distance of center of mass movement vary considerably among players." Nevertheless, there is no exact way to measure how wide your stance should be; you will discover your ideal width only by experimenting.

With longer clubs, take a wider stance, which allows for a greater shift in your center of gravity and produces a wider swing arc, yielding additional clubhead speed. Adopting a narrower stance with your wedge or short irons will encourage a smaller shift in your center of gravity and a steeper angle of attack—both of which will help you precisely control clubhead speed, which is more important than generating maximum speed on every swing. A steeper angle of attack increases backspin, making the ball stop nearer its point of landing.

Matching the width of your stance to the club in your hands brings you closer to your ultimate objective: maximum distance with woods and more precise control of clubhead speed for accuracy with irons.

Taking It on the Golf Course: The Weight Shift Exercise

This drill will help you keep your weight on the balls of the feet. It also will help you discover a desirable rhythm, for a stress-free swing that is easy on the back.

Here's how to perform this simple exercise:

1. Start with your feet close together.

2. Make a step onto your back foot and swing the club back.

3. Swing through, finishing balanced on your forward foot.

WEIGHT SHIFT EXERCISE

Part II

The Short Game

Where Art Meets Science

WE ALL MARVEL AT SHORT-GAME WIZARDS who can outscore stronger, more athletic opponents. Ego-satisfying as it is to hit thunderbolts off the tee and high, arching irons, the short game—representing roughly 60 percent of the shots we play—is key to low scoring. If you compare two equally skilled golfers, it is usually the golfer who can't sink his three-foot putts or escape from greenside bunkers who pays the tab on the nineteenth hole.

Many golfers have the misimpression that the short game requires a knack or "touch" that one is either born with or not. Often they've convinced themselves of this after trying—and abandoning—any number of training aids purporting to help them chip, pitch, or putt.

I can help you dramatically improve your short game through technique. To do that, you must first grasp two critical, often neglected but easy-to-understand elements of the short game: how the power is generated, and how it is controlled.

Almost all shots around the green are mechanically straightforward. The art lies in the imagination—the creativity—to visualize the necessary carry, roll, and pace. Watching Seve Ballesteros or Tiger Woods work wonders around the green leaves no doubt that an exceptional short game melds both right and left hemispheres of the brain. And proper mechanics are the first step. As author and acting coach Joseph Chaikin said, "Technique is a means to free the artist."

MOTION AND MOMENTUM: THE PURE FLOW OF MOMENTUM AND GRAVITY

When you're putting and chipping, your torso, shoulders, and arms move in unison, to the rhythm of a pendulum. The lower body stays "quiet." In the longer swing of the pitch and sand shot, the hips and legs will rotate in unison with the upper body to accommodate a greater range of motion.

Many of my students are quite surprised at this difference, especially as it relates to the pitch shot. They think of a pitch as essentially a full swing made with a wedge, so they decelerate before impact, creating the desired clubhead speed with their muscles. Not at all reliable or precise, this approach will result in a life sentence of mediocrity.

The energy required of the club to move the ball from A to B should come from the natural forces of gravity and momentum. A stroke that integrates these two forces produces a precise amount of clubhead speed. You can control this speed by simply altering the length of the swing based on the distance your shot must travel. The beauty of this technique is certainty and repeatability, for gravity is unfailing and exact. This is the reason so much emphasis is given to the pendulum motion. It alone is the source of precision.

To hit short-game shots the desired distance, you need only control the length of the stroke—that is, the arc the clubhead travels. I'm going to show you how to do just that for each of the short-game strokes.

MAKE GRAVITY YOUR BEST FRIEND— SHE'LL ALWAYS BE THERE

In the short game, the power you generate will be directly proportional to how far back you take the clubhead before you let it begin its pendulum-like descent. Following Newton's law, gravity alone will provide the necessary acceleration.

According to Newton, objects accelerate as they fall through space. If you drop a stone from a third-floor window, it will be traveling faster when it hits the ground than if you drop it from the second floor.

5
PUTTING

TO PUTT WELL, YOU NEED to send the ball consistently along the target line for the intended distance. To do that means making use of gravity and momentum—not muscular action—to control clubhead speed.

Letting gravity do the work is actually much easier than what most players do. The most common mistake I see in putting is players trying to guide or control the putter by coordinating a complex muscle action of their forearms, hands, and wrists. Now and then they'll have hot streaks, but they're rarely consistent, and they're never quite sure what they did that worked.

If this describes your approach, you will probably admit to an underlying feeling of insecurity when approaching the green. What can you expect? There are just too many variables entered into your putting equation to perform well consistently, especially when the pressure is on.

Here's how to develop a putting stroke you can trust. I'll start with the overall motion before showing you how to set up, grip the club, and aim. Just as with the full swing, I've found that if you first understand the motion—what parts of your body move through space—it will be much easier to see how all the other elements fit.

THE PERFECT PUTTING MOTION

Our objective is to make the stroke as simple as possible, to eliminate variables that stand in the way of our quest for precision. Only your upper body moves in putting. Imagine your lower body as a pillar, stationary and stable.

You can quickly get a feel for this motion—upper body moving, lower body still—even if you don't have a putter nearby.

Putting Motion Exercise

The following exercise is an easy way to experience the isolation of your upper body. I have all my students do this without a golf club. Ideally you should try this with a medicine ball, but if you don't have one handy as you are reading this, you can use instead a nearby vase or an unabridged dictionary. Make a motion like rocking a baby, using only your upper body. Imagine your body starting from the rib cage and moving up through your shoulders.

Longer-shafted "belly putters" have been popular on tour lately for a couple of good reasons. This style of putter demands a unified motion of the arms and shoulders, eliminating excessive hand action. Whether you are partial to this style of putter or not, you don't have to go out and purchase one to experience its benefits. If you have a putter handy, try this exercise (shown in the top sequence on the facing page). Place the butt of the putter's shaft against your belly button and clasp your hands together on the shaft itself. Perform your putting stroke, making sure that the butt of the club remains in your belly. (Any hinging of the wrists during the stroke should be passive.)

This is such a great drill for practicing your putting motion that you might want to incorporate it into your preround warm-up.

Then, as shown in the sequence below, simply drop the putter while maintaining your posture and continue the same motion. *Voilà, you now have a quality putting stroke!*

After you have completed your stroke, turn your head to look at the hole to see the result.

I've started with and emphasized the motion of your putting stroke because it is the one element that can't vary if you are to achieve consistency. Some of the other elements are more variable.

SETUP

Posture

If you watch the pros warming up on the putting green before any professional tournament, you'll be amazed at how different their postures are when addressing the ball. Posture, or how to stand, involves a large dose of personal preference.

Several great putters, like Jack Nicklaus, hunch over until their shoulders are nearly horizontal to the ground. Others, like Tiger Woods, maintain a more straightly aligned spinal column, more akin to their full swing posture.

Each posture dictates a slightly different motion of the putter, and each has its advantages and drawbacks. I'll explain them here, and tell you what I prefer, but you should experiment and use whatever posture works best for you.

Putting with a curved spine. Although this involves a considerable forward curve of the spine, it actually promotes a straighter path along the target line. With this posture, the blade rotates less relative to the target line. It is less "open and close," more "square to square." However, it is a challenge to find and replicate this posture each time you address the ball.

Putting with a straight spine. I think this posture is easier to repeat and more similar to a normal swing posture. One arguable disadvantage is that your putter will swing on more of an arc relative to the target line, with considerable rotation of the clubface, so your stroke's timing and tempo must be good.

Whether you bend forward with a straight spine or a more relaxed curvature depends entirely on what feels more comfortable to you.

Grip

If you watch the pros, you'll also see a good deal of variation in how they grip the putter. The vast majority who apply a more conventional grip share one element in common: their palms face off in direct opposition to each other, with neither hand in a dominant position. This is done to pre-

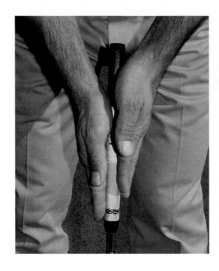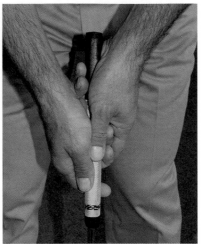

vent the clubface from twisting or turning during the stroke, and avoids a tendency to pull the clubface off its natural arc line. Just as you don't want to drive a car that has a front end alignment problem, you don't want to use your putter with one!

To consistently find the appropriate hand position, just clasp your palms together initially, as shown above, and then take your grip.

BALL PLACEMENT

There are various theories on where in your pendulum arc you should make contact with the ball.

The very lowest point of the arc or ever so slightly on the upstroke is the most reliable (although there have been some very good putters who claim to make contact on the way down). If you make contact as your clubface is descending, it may generate backspin; the inverse seems logical as well—an ascending clubface will generate topspin. Of course, whatever helps the ball roll truer when it touches is the desired objective.

To get that result, take a shoulder-width stance and place the ball somewhere between your sternum and just a couple of inches in front. This will result in contact occurring just as your putter ascends from the lowest point of the stroke.

Equally important is where you make contact with the ball. Research by Dave Peltz shows that the ratio of skid to roll decreases (the ball starts rolling sooner) if you contact the ball above its equator.

AIM

One common and easily correctable mistake I see in putting stems from poor alignment.

Just as with the full swing, you want your putter's face pointing at the target with your feet parallel to this line. This means that when positioned correctly, your feet will actually be pointing left of your intended target.

One distinct advantage of putting is that you are able to pick up, clean, and then place the ball. As most instructors will tell you, this

On target.

Off line.

provides the opportunity to line up the ball to the hole with the ball's writing or a drawn line. I suggest you do so.

Taking It on the Golf Course: Learning Distance Control

Line up several balls in relation to a hole, allow-  ing a couple of feet to separate each one. Starting with the shortest putt, proceed through the line of balls, progressively lengthening your backswing with each putt. You will quickly learn the relation- ship between stroke length and distance. Further- more, since not all greens are the same speed, this drill is great for calibrating your stroke to the speed of the greens before going out to play. You should start on a level surface and then progress to uphill, downhill, right to left, and left to right.

On fast greens you may stroke a downhill twenty-footer like a three-footer . . . and vice versa. For breaking putts, you will notice that as you progress farther from the hole, the amount of break that you must account for increases. So if you are aiming an inch outside the hole from four feet away, you may have to allow for a six-inch break from twelve feet away. There is no perfect formula for figuring out the exact amount of break needed. It depends on the speed of the green and the severity of the slope. Experience will be your best teacher, helping you develop an innate sense of the stroke length required for a given putt, otherwise known as "feel."

With each successive putt you simply lengthen your backswing. In the picture opposite, I had lined up five balls with about two feet separating each one. I asked Nicolas Haro, my photographer, to take a picture of the stroke of each putt. Depicted below is the actual stroke length of putts number 1 and 5. As you will clearly see, the amplitude of the stroke has increased dramatically, perhaps doubled.

The stroke of putt number 1, a distance of three feet from the hole.

The stroke of putt number 5, a distance of fifteen feet from the hole.

6
CHIPPING

CHIPPING IS CALLED FOR when your ball is just off the green and must traverse a short distance where fringe or rough might slow it down, knock it off course, or stop it completely. In these situations, you need to get the ball airborne with a lofted club so that it lands on the green and rolls to the hole like a putt. You do this with a stroke that is similar to your putting stroke, with a few modifications in setup.

The club you chip with depends largely on your lie and distance from the hole. The ratio of carry and roll will be determined by the loft of the club you choose. Elect one of your wedges for most shots around the green, but learn to use a less lofted club—e.g., a 7, 8, or 9 iron—for longer distance and roll. You can add a 3- or 4-wood option to your chipping arsenal/repertoire, as the ball will roll more like a putt, skipping the first couple of feet through whatever fringe before rolling toward the hole. If you limit yourself to a few clubs, it will be easier to learn to make an educated guess about the stroke necessary for the shot. The practice drill on page 59 will acquaint you with the carry and roll of each club.

MOTION

Chipping, like putting, requires a stationary lower body. Your torso and arms move in sync, promoting the same pendulum flow of the clubface as in putting.

As in putting, you want to eliminate any active wrist action. This action interrupts the natural flow of momentum, and it also changes the path of the clubhead. Instead of contact occurring as the clubhead descends, flicking the wrists takes the club out of your intended arc and on a different path to the ball. With longer chipping strokes a certain degree of natural hinge of the wrists will occur on the backswing if your hands and wrists are relaxed. This is okay and a natural reaction to greater momentum generated.

As the saying goes, "Let the club do the work." Gravity and the natural generation of momentum is all you need. But the setup for chipping involves two important modifications in your putting stroke, in terms of the angle of the shaft and where you place the ball in your stance.

SETUP

For most chip shots, you will do well contacting the ball with a slightly descending blow. A common mistake is to try to lift the ball or make a level strike, instead of contacting the ball on the descending part of the arc of your stroke. You can achieve the correct downward action simply by placing the ball farther back in your stance, *at a point in the arc where the clubface is still descending slightly and hasn't quite reached its lowest point.* Every stroke you make should have a natural arc, so instead of trying to hit down on the ball, you need only place the ball in the appropriate position.

As I said, the stroke is similar to putting, with two important modifications in setup.

1. *Ball position.* Position the ball farther back in your stance, a couple of inches behind the center of your sternum (which marks your center point). If you feel more comfortable with a wider putting stance, this will be only slightly back of center. If you prefer a narrow stance, position the ball opposite your right foot. If the ball is "sitting up," meaning it is not lying firmly on the ground but is propped up by the grass as if on a short tee, this is an opportunity to play it more forward in your stance and stroke it exactly like a putt. See "Analyzing Your Lie," page 64.

2. *Shaft.* The combination of your hands set forward and the ball positioned back creates a forward-leaning shaft, as shown in the first frame on page 58. Note how in the bottom left frame the club returns to contact the ball at the same forward-leaning angle it was at address.

Resist your natural inclination to watch the ball an instant after impact; observe instead, in the sequence below, how my head does not move until the very last frame.

WEIGHT SHIFT

As in putting, you don't want any weight shift when you chip. Any shifting of your center of gravity or movement of your spine will adversely affect the precision and repeatability of your stroke. See the special drill on page 109.

Exercise: Covering the Distances

The photo sequence below shows a drill for systematically practicing all the range of distances you will face from off the green. Conceptually, it is nothing more than a variation of the drill for putting. As in the putting drill, you practice the entire range of strokes. By lengthening your backswing with each successive stroke, you will witness each ball travel and roll a little farther.

You can also try a variation of this drill: start by placing balls off the green spaced at increasing distances from the hole. Begin with the ball

closest to the hole and progressively lengthen your backswing as you go. You will quickly learn the all-important direct relationship between distance and stroke length as you watch each ball carry and roll farther.

Direct observation and experimentation develop "feel," an innate sense of the stroke required for the particular shot at hand.

Effective chipping involves accounting for two key variables that will determine how your chip reacts after landing:

1. **The hardness of the surface** on which the ball lands affects the crucial first "bounce."

2. **The speed of the green** determines how it will "roll out" after landing. This speed is measured by the so-called Stimp rating.

These two variables have nothing to do with your stroke mechanics. This drill will allow you to experience these variables and adjust your stroke and club selection before facing the first chip shot on the course.

As you play different golf courses, you will encounter greens that are firm or soft, or fast or slow. Even on the same course, meteorological factors and greenskeeping result in changing conditions from day to day, green to green.

This drill provides a perfect way to test the greens of the course you are playing and adjust/calibrate your stroke before playing. It will boost your confidence to judge speeds early in the round, and reduce guesswork. Try moving around to different points on the green and let this "squadron" approach help you learn to attack the hole from every angle.

7
PITCHING

IF YOU KNOW WHAT YOU'RE DOING, pitching is a wondrous delight. If you don't, it can be the bane of your golfing existence!

A pitching stroke is called for when the ball lies within approximately fifty yards of the green, the shot requiring more carry than roll. A thirty- or forty-yard carry is too much distance for your chipping stroke to cover. Even if you could cover that distance by chipping with a low lofted club, e.g., a 6 or 7 iron, you do not always have the luxury of a virtual runway between you and the hole allowing for a terrestrial approach.

Pitching with a high lofted club lets you get the ball airborne more easily, fly it a longer distance, and land it softly on the green. As in chipping, which club to use depends on your lie and distance from the hole. By practicing with only a couple of different clubs, such as a sand wedge and a 9 iron, you will become accustomed to their general carry-and-roll characteristics. By following the practice drill shown on page 65, you'll soon learn to gauge the right club and stroke length required for different situations.

LEARN THE MOTION

In pitching, your body, arms, and club move in unison, like a pendulum. The length of the stroke increases the clubhead speed generated. The motion is similar to a simple underhand toss, as shown in the sequence below. Indeed, achieving consistency relies on employing forces that are repeatable. Passive hands are better than controlling ones.

Anybody can do this!

SETUP

Posture. As in your full swing, bend from the hips and flex your knees.

It's critical that *your arms hang closer to your body than in the regular golf swing.* Let your arms hang to a nearly vertical position. This proximity permits a more unified motion of body, arms, and club. Note below how at address and impact the arms hang straight down from the shoulders. This is a critical distinction from the full swing, as you will note when comparing the arm position for a full swing on page 22. In pitching, gravity more than centrifugal force is at play.

Alignment. Whether you set up open or square for a pitch shot, your hips and upper body should be aligned perfectly. This alignment promotes the unity of their action. If they are not aligned, they work against each other, creating unnecessary and incalculable amounts of torque. Your arc will be inconsistent as well.

WEIGHT SHIFT

As in chipping and putting, there is no need to shift your weight when you pitch. Except in extreme cases, enough clubhead speed is generated for nearly all shots around the green with the simple turn of your body. Take a narrow stance, to deter any weight shift. While you're learning this, the narrower the better, as any shifting will cause you to lose your balance (see drill on page 111).

DISTANCE CONTROL

Learning the relationship between swing length and distance is the same for pitching as it was for putting and chipping, except you are making longer swings. The greater the length of the pendulum arc made by the clubhead, the greater the clubhead speed and, hence, the greater the distance. Distances become a basic mathematic equation: think of your upswing as your input, the downswing as your output.

You will note that the pendulum-like action is consistent throughout the entire short game, as shown in the drill on the facing page.

ANALYZING YOUR LIE: A KEY TO PRECISION CHIPPING AND PITCHING

You can significantly improve your shot making by knowing how the ball's lie affects the requirements of your shot making. Once you know what you are looking for, you'll be in a much better position to make the necessary adjustments. (Although I've placed this in the short-game section, it is equally valid for full-swing iron shots.)

9 o'clock: 30 yards.

10 o'clock: 40 yards.

11 o'clock: 50 yards.

A first step in analyzing a lie is to imagine the clubhead's traditional path to the ball and what the clubface will encounter along its way. As you see below, with the ball "sitting up" you are able to strike it more directly with no loss of energy or distance. However, when the ball is "sitting down" (in the photo on the right), considerable grass will come between the clubhead and the ball. A usual approach to the ball will meet with potential disaster, so you must take another path. This path is a sharper angle, whereby less grass will come between your clubface and the ball.

Ball sitting up.

Ball sitting down.

Ball sitting up. When there is grass propping your ball up from the ground's hard surface, it is, technically speaking, "sitting up." It's easier to make solid contact with the ball from this type of lie because the natural arc of your stroke will give the face a more direct approach to the ball. You won't be required, as when the ball is sitting down, to strike with a more descending blow.

Here's how to execute the shot when the ball is sitting up:

- **Setup:** Play the ball more forward in your stance, closer to your front foot (see the first frame on the following page).

- **Spin:** Note that the shaft leans in a neutral, almost vertical position (not leaning forward or back) at address and impact. The ball is farther forward in the arc of your stroke, so the angle of attack is shallower, *producing less backspin* (especially if there's grass between the clubhead and your ball). However, you can easily *create more loft* from this lie by opening your clubface, so as to make the ball land softly (otherwise known as a "flop" shot).

Full pitch sequence: ball sitting up.

- **Stroke length:** Because the ball is sitting up, the club encounters little resistance through the impact zone, so the *follow-through is nearly identical in length to the backswing,* a picture of symmetry between the top of the stroke and the finish.

Ball sitting down. Your ball is "sitting down" when there is little if any grass between it and the ground, but potentially much between the club-face and the ball. This lie creates both a challenge and an opportunity.

The challenge is that it requires a steeper angle of attack. If the ball were sitting down the fairway, known as a "tight lie," you could generate backspin on the shot, helpful when the ball must stop quickly upon landing.

Here's how to execute the shot when the ball is sitting down:

- **Setup:** Play the ball farther back in your stance to ensure contact earlier in the arc, when the club is on a steep descent (see the first frame on the facing page).

- **Spin:** Note that at impact the shaft is leaning slightly forward, indicating a downward blow, the ball being compressed against the club and turf. A tightly cropped fairway is an opportunity to create some *backspin.* If, however, your ball is sitting down in the rough, grass will likely get in between your ball and the clubhead, eliminating any spin.

- **Stroke length:** Never try to force a follow-through to match your backswing. (In fact, you will be surprised how abbreviated your follow-through may be, and it will vary with every shot, depending on the amount of resistance the clubhead encounters on its path through impact.) In the pictures below, note the asymmetry between backswing length and follow-through, as the club encounters more natural resistance from the ground.

Full pitch sequence: ball sitting down.

8
SAND PLAY

DEVELOPING A SWING YOU CAN TRUST from a sand trap is much easier than most people realize. That's because the mechanics of the swing from the sand are identical to the pitch stroke in every way, with just a few important modifications in the setup.

Many students come to me having been taught the right basics— open the clubface and "hit the sand two inches behind the ball." This may even work for a while, but eventually, not understanding the key elements, players start to try actively controlling the club instead of letting the club move through its natural pendulum arc. They might attempt several different approaches, but never feel confident that any particular one will work consistently.

When you get into a trap, I want you to think of yourself as just having to play another pitch shot. Here's how.

The motion: Just as in pitching, your arms and the club move together like a pendulum, the length of which varies according to the length of the shot. The longer the stroke, the more clubhead speed generated.

SETUP

Ball position. In properly executed sand shots, the clubface never touches the ball.

Therefore, the ball should be played more forward in your stance than a pitch shot. Opposite the middle of your left foot, well ahead of the bottom of your stroke, is a good starting point. The ball's position should always be forward of the lowest point of your arc so that the clubhead contacts the sand first.

Unfortunately, many players make the shot harder than it is by playing the ball too far back in the stance. They attempt to hit a spot behind the ball, rather than simply playing the ball forward and routinely hitting the sand first! Not only does this require extraordinary hand-eye coordination, but it forces you to change your natural motion as you attempt to hit the "right spot" behind the ball. Putting the ball forward in your stance makes this far less complicated. It reduces the "fear factor," allowing you to swing freely and finish comfortably balanced on your left side.

Stance. When a pro gets into a bunker, you always see him dig in with his feet. The reason to do this is not just to gain a more secure stance, but to embed your feet so they are a shade lower than the ball. This will help you hit under the ball, creating an explosion of sand rather than striking the ball itself. So dig in. Open your stance so that it points left of the target; open your clubface about the same degree right of the target.

Note the forward ball position, weight forward, and finish forward in this sequence.

Shaft angle and sand wedge design. If you are playing in soft sand, the clubface will zip through the sand more easily if the shaft is in a neutral position, not leaning forward, as in a traditional iron shot. Every sand wedge is designed with a certain degree of "bounce"—the amount of metal that bulges below the leading edge. The "bounce" helps the club-head slide along and move through the sand and prevents the leading edge from digging too deeply into the sand. Use this to your advantage.

A CLOSER LOOK

With the ball positioned forward in the stance, the club's first and only contact is sand. Supported by a mass of movement of sand underneath, like a djinni on a Persian rug, the ball is carried toward its intended destination.

Part III

Special Shots and Drills

9
SITUATIONS

. . . A FAIRWAY BUNKER

The word *bunker* suggests a difficult and penalizing situation. In actuality, a fairway bunker is not a difficult shot from a mechanical perspective, but one requiring more precision, some imagination, and a little experience.

Unlike with traditional greenside bunker shots, precision is required to contact the ball first, and *then* the sand. You only have to catch a little sand before impact, and the ball travels half the distance. Therefore, fairway bunkers are a pure test in ball striking.

Make sure you hit the ball first, *and then sand.*

You are not allowed to ground your club, so it should hover just above the sand at address position.

It is easy to be distracted and unnerved by all the sand surrounding your ball. Therefore, use the power of your imagination to envision the surface of the sand as green, as though the ball were sitting in the fairway. Your imagination helps you to summon up the correct order of contact—that is, ball, then sand.

. . . UNDER THE TREES

Trajectory and length of swing are key!

Hitting the ball on a low trajectory for a distance less than one hundred yards is a much easier shot than most people realize. The key is to *apply the mechanics of your pitching stroke with a less lofted club.* Depending on how low you need to hit the ball and how far you have to go, you can choose anything from an 8 iron to your 3 iron to a hybrid. Choke down on the club so that it is the same length as your wedge.

To perfect this new shot, practice on the range to gain a precise idea of the trajectory and how much carry and roll you'll get with a couple of different clubs. Practice the entire range of backstrokes (i.e., 9, 10, and 11 o'clock).

If you intend to hit the ball more than a hundred yards, position the ball back in your stance and make a three-quarter swing.

WHEN IN TROUBLE, PLAY THE PERCENTAGES

If you think a 7 iron will keep the ball just under those branches, it is better to use a 5 or 6 iron just to be sure. (Just as if you think you can go over trees with a 7 iron, take an 8 or 9 iron instead.) This approach simply increases the probability of your success and helps you avoid disastrous consequences. Remember, golf is a thinking game, so decision making is often as important as swing.

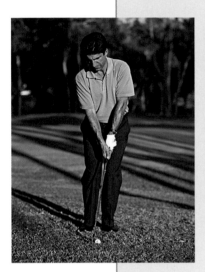

. . . OVER WATER, TREES, OR BUILDINGS

Driving over water or hitting an iron to a heavily guarded green is just as much about mental game as about swing mechanics.

Making one's best swing when faced with a threatening situation is a challenge to all players, but some are able to do it regularly. We have all witnessed talented players crack under tournament pressure, or even seen ourselves fold in a Nassau game with friends. I asked Arlene McKitrick, whom I have the pleasure of coaching, to take this shot as a testament to her mental fortitude. She has an unbelievable knack for winning, having more victories than any other female amateur in the history of golf.

She often faces daunting situations like this long carry over water on the fifth hole at Longboat Key Club. So what exactly is her thought process? In Arlene's words: "I have a fear of failing just like anybody else, but I employ some mental techniques that can work for you. There is tremendous power in Imagineering. So imagine that you were already

successful in executing the shot, that you have hit your target area. If you act fearful and worry about the water, that fear will overtake the power of your target. So you really need to focus on your landing area to block out the fear. Your vision will tell your body what it has to do to accomplish the desired result."

. . . DIFFERENT LIES

Play the ball farther back in your stance when it's sitting down, farther forward when up. The former will result in more of a downward blow, the shaft leaning toward the target, and the latter a shallower blow, with the shaft in a neutral position. This change in strike is best achieved by altering ball position rather than by radically changing your swing.

Whenever much grass is likely to get between your clubhead and the ball at impact, it's called a "flier." As the term implies, the ball will often fly longer and with less spin, making it more difficult to control distance. Allow for this by taking one less club (e.g., a 7 instead of a 6 iron) or a shorter backswing.

The flight characteristics of a ball sitting tight to the fairway are the reverse—it will fly less and spin more. Expert players often prefer this kind of lie with their irons because it gives them more ability to stop the ball close to a tightly guarded pin. As you improve, you can prove this to yourself by hitting several balls to a vacant green from the two lies. Your distance control is likely to be better from the tighter lie. Nevertheless, proper contact with a ball "sitting down" requires a greater degree of swing precision—missing only marginally fat or thin will result in greater error.

. . . Ball sitting up.

. . . *Ball sitting down.*

. . . DIFFERENT SLOPES

Swinging on a slope requires adjustments in your setup, swing motion, and club selection. The correct adjustments will allow you to make solid contact with the ball and achieve proper shot distance.

A more severe slope requires a greater adjustment in setup and swing motion. I have purposefully chosen dramatic slopes to clearly illustrate this, and have divided them into two categories: "up and down" and "sidehills."

In both uphill and downhill lies, you want to set *your spine angle perpendicular to the slope* (or if you prefer, *shoulders parallel to the slope*). This alters the approach of your clubface, so that it encounters the ball squarely instead of colliding with the hillside. In the photo sequences on pages 86–87, note the way that I hold a club parallel to my shoulders across my chest: from this position, you can practice your rotation until you become comfortable. You should then take a couple of practice swings to accurately identify the precise angle necessary.

Your swing motion will be affected by the slope. Depending on the slope's severity, a normal weight shift and finish may be impossible. On more extreme slopes, maintain your balance throughout the entire motion on the inside of the downhill foot (i.e., right foot on upslopes, left foot on downslopes). In the photo sequences, you will note that my center of gravity appears significantly farther back than usual and that I achieve a more abbreviated finish. While this setup and motion are not as pretty as a full golf swing, they work to enable you to get the best result. Your best shot making will be produced by solid ball contact and staying balanced.

You will also need to modify your club selection when swinging on slopes. Swinging on an upslope will increase the trajectory of your shot and thus make your ball carry a shorter distance. An 8 iron's flight can resemble that of a wedge, which for some players will carry about 135 yards instead of the usual 150. This same effect is produced around the green: a pitch shot made with a sand wedge will travel higher and shorter than normal, as if the loft were a lob wedge. You will need, therefore, to make a longer swing or use a less lofted club. The opposite holds true for downslopes: swinging will decrease the trajectory of your shot and thus make your ball carry a greater distance. As necessary, you should make a shorter swing or use a more lofted club.

Note to the beginner: In your first month or two of playing golf, I recommend you practice on level ground while you are "grooving" your swing. As your swing develops, you will be ready to incorporate the changes that various slopes present.

UPHILL

- Consider choosing a slightly less lofted club to account for higher trajectory.

- Tilt until you are parallel to the slope, your center of gravity back in your stance.

- Maintain your posture through the swing.

DOWNHILL

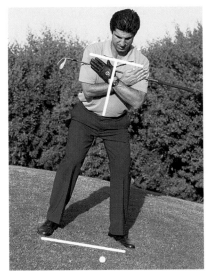 

- Choose a slightly more lofted club to account for lower trajectory.

- Tilt until you are parallel to the slope and set your center of gravity forward in your stance.

- Maintain your posture through the swing.

From sidehill lies, you must adjust your primary spinal tilt by standing more erect when the ball is above your feet, and bending over more when the ball is below your feet. The common tendency, because of muscle memory, is to unconsciously return to your habitual impact position when swinging. In order to resist this, you have to become familiar with these unusual postures, which you can do by making a couple of practice swings.

One simple, helpful way to remember this is to "stay tall" when the ball is above your feet and "stay low" and over the ball when it's below.

BALL ABOVE YOUR FEET: "START TALL, STAY TALL"

- Stand taller at address and maintain your height throughout the swing, particularly through impact.

- Allow for the ball to move to the left, by aiming slightly to the right of your intended target.

BALL BELOW YOUR FEET: "START LOW, STAY LOW"

- Bend over more at address with more knee flex until your clubface is grounded.

- Allow for the ball to move a little to the right by aligning slightly left of your target.

- Maintain your angles throughout the swing, especially through impact.

. . . DEEP ROUGH

Long grass has the effect of closing the face of the club and decreasing its loft. Thus, you will want to use a more lofted club than if the ball were in the fairway. Your first consideration should be getting the ball out of the rough. If you have a long distance left to play, use of lofted fairway woods or a hybrid club is advisable if the lie permits. The long grass will decrease the loft of these clubs, and the ball may actually go the distance you would expect if you were using the less lofted fairway woods. When in very deep rough, use a more lofted club. The deepest rough shots are custom-made for a sand or lob wedge, especially when the grass is as long and thick, as shown in the photo below.

The best technique for successfully extricating yourself from this predicament involves two important modifications to your swing. Quickly and fully break your wrists—as I demonstrate below—even in a half-swing, which "steepens" your angle of attack, so the club approaches from a sharper, more direct angle, getting more ball and less grass. This helps you avoid most of the grass that you would encounter with your usual approach.

Note how the clubface stays "open" at the finish, leaving the back of the left hand pointing at the sky.

. . . ADVERSE WEATHER CONDITIONS

Unless you live in southern California or northern Australia, you should be prepared to play in rain, wind, or cold. Even a "fair weather" player will face a sudden change in conditions.

One of my favorite students, Avron Brog, who took up golf at sixty-five, has a toughness and determination second to none. "There is no such thing as bad weather," he would say, "only inappropriate clothing." Being comfortable and being warm are essential to executing your best golf swing. I like the challenge of battling with Mother Nature—though perhaps not as much as Avron—and you will play better and be more comfortable if you know how to prepare.

Here are some suggestions and simple considerations for dress for performing your best under various conditions:

Cold: Layer your clothing. Try a thin layer of long underwear—silk or any of the breathable, moisture-wicking synthetic fabrics. This is one great tour player secret worth sharing! You can add one or two more layers, a turtleneck wool sweater and a sleeveless vest, depending how cold it is. Keeping your hands warm is another priority. Winter gloves and warmers are made by several manufacturers.

Wind: Absolutely wear a *wind-protective outer layer* to protect yourself. A sweater is definitely not a "windbreaker" as such.

Rain: I strongly recommend you invest in quality rainwear. Staying dry and having your swing unrestricted is possible with today's outerwear fabrics. Now, nearly soundless, lightweight material is available in many attractive styles and colors. As any experienced hiker will tell you, *do not wear cotton*, which absorbs moisture. To complete your "suit of armor," a pair of rain gloves will help you keep a solid grip on the club. In fact, they become more adhesive as your grip's surface gets wet.

10
DRILLS FOR SKILL DEVELOPMENT

ANY EXERCISE OR DRILL SHOULD BE JUDGED by its ability to achieve measurable results. The drills in this section will help you solve certain technical problems, refine specific elements of your game, and support your general development of strength, coordination, and alignment. Use them in your training sessions, as they will keep you on the fast track to becoming a complete player.

1. PERFECT AIM

Alignment problems are natural to *all golfers.* On several occasions, I have corrected alignment problems of professional players, who are not immune to elementary problems. Any misalignment requires even the most skilled player to make adjustments in their swing to compensate.

On the driving range, you can "train your eyes" by placing two clubs parallel—one along your stance line, in front of your toes, and the other outside the ball on the target line, as shown in the top photo on page 94. You can also place a third club to check where you have the ball placed in your stance.

Nick Price commented that during his most torrid stretch of golf, alignment was his only concern. Brent Robinson also places a high priority on alignment. Says Brent, "Roberto regularly reminds me that in order to perform my best, I need to be just as meticulous with my alignment as I am with my swing." You can check your alignment when you

As seen here from two angles, Brent's clubs are laid out like railroad tracks.

are practicing or warming up on the range, as shown in the photos at the bottom of the facing page, without any devices or special technology.

Once you are properly aligned you may be in for a surprise. You may well feel like you are aimed way left or right of your target. Patience is a virtue here, and knowing that, with a short passage of time your perception will *gradually* adjust to "see correctly."

Regularly check your alignment when practicing on the range. Just remember that your trusted swing is most effective when your aim is on.

BRENT ROBINSON is a golf professional from South Africa who currently divides his time between the United Kingdom and the United States. Brent earned his playing privileges for the Euro Pro Tour this year and looks forward to competing.

2. LEVERAGING YOUR POWER

Players benefit from swinging a heavy club, helping them develop a swing that is "on plane" and maximally leveraged. Unless you took up golf at a tender age when the club was heavy relative to your body weight, identifying the ideal space through which to swing the club is a challenge. You can enjoy the same developmental progress of a youngster by training with a specially weighted golf club or even with five- or ten-pound weight plates from your gym.

Arlene McKitrick comments, "This is one of several drills from my training sessions with Roberto that have increased the power and efficiency of my swing, and definitely brought my game to the next level."

ARLENE MCKITRICK has won more tournaments than any other female amateur in history, including a record forty-four straight World Senior titles. Despite a long battle with type I diabetes, she continues to improve on an already brilliant career, winning championships at prestigious clubs such as Congressional CC, the TPC Prestancia, and Longboat Key Club. She recently shot a 65 at the Ritz Golf Club in Sarasota, besting the previous record held by touring pro Paul Azinger. When not traveling to tournaments, Arlene and her husband, John, spend the summers in Ohio and the winters in Longboat Key, Florida.

3. COORDINATION AND SWING DYNAMICS: "SHIFT AND TURN"

The correct move from the top of the swing is not a simple turn of the hips, as many believe. Instead, a slight lateral shift should initiate the downswing, *and then a turn.* This is the move of all effective swings on both the women's and men's tours.

This challenging exercise will develop your coordination and, most uniquely, ensure the right dynamic and sequence in your swing.

Keije Isobe, an eleven handicap, who is playing the best golf of his life as a senior, credits this exercise for his success and demonstrates below. First assume your normal setup position. Then step back with your front foot on the backswing, balancing inside your right instep. To initiate the move down, step forward and feel your weight move to a point inside your left foot. From there, you pivot and strike the ball with effortless power.

"I first thought Roberto was crazy when he showed me this exercise, but now I thank him. I hit the ball farther now," says Keije. "I had reached a plateau in my golf game for several years, but I have suddenly gained fifteen to twenty yards off the tee! More importantly, I have an understanding and feeling for the right swing mechanics. My only regret is my Nassau partners in the United States and Japan will know my secret."

Instead of shifting, then turning, "slicers" do just the opposite, turning immediately to start the downswing. This produces an out-to-in swing path, and a slice (or a pull, if you manage to square the clubface).

Good players demonstrate a balanced and definitive shift at the beginning of the downswing onto the inside of their left foot. This smooth move forward allows the arms to drop back toward the body and along the correct path inside the target line.

Feel that you initiate the start of your downswing by moving your hips forward toward the target. So incorporate this move, popularly referred to by tour players as "the bump," and begin your downswing by moving your hips forward toward the target. If you keep your upper body relaxed, your arms will drop and begin their descent on the right path, from where you can swing as aggressively as you like.

KEIJE ISOBE is a native of Osaka, Japan, and resides in New York, where he runs a fashion company and is an active supporter of many charities.

4. ARC CONSISTENCY: WITH THE ONE-ARM SWING

The consistency of your swing arc requires the development of stability and strength in your left side. Your left side establishes the true arc of your swing, since your left hand is the last contact with the club. I often tell my players to "listen to your left." The left side is usually the weaker side of the right-handed golfer. Consequently, most amateurs suffer from an overly dominant right side, which overtakes the left, throwing the club off plane and the swing off-kilter. (Your dominant side usually corresponds with your writing hand.)

This drill will help you strengthen your left side and experience swing sensation as many great players describe it—as a power-supplying right side working within the structure of a fully extended, firm, stable left side.

Belen Mozo beautifully demonstrates the "left-arm-only swing" on the following page. Make a swing holding the club only with your weaker hand (usually the left), placing your dominant hand behind your back. You will quickly and progressively strengthen your weaker side. This drill produces additional benefits, as well—it helps you find the

right rhythm and requires you to respect the natural flow of momentum on the downswing.

Belen: "This exercise will help you develop left-side strength and better rhythm, important elements for consistent, solid ball contact. It is a great exercise to incorporate into your practice sessions and to turn to on days when you may be trying to overpower the ball. It helps you stay with the natural momentum without overpowering your swing with your dominant side."

BELEN MOZO is a native of Spain. Just seventeen years old, she has won several prestigious international golf tournaments, including the 2006 British Amateur. She made the cut in the Women's British Open playing as an amateur in her first professional tournament. The recipient of a full golf scholarship, she attends the University of California in Los Angeles.

5. "STEP AND SWING":
FOR BALANCE AND RHYTHM

As a six-time World Long Drive Championship finalist, Davyn Nola has an extraordinary ability to generate power. He holds New Zealand's Long Drive Record of 428 yards, but like many other big-hitters, he also works on hitting it straighter.

"Since working with Roberto, I'm hitting the ball longer and *straighter!*" exclaims Davyn. "This drill in particular helped my balance, rhythm, and timing considerably, all crucial factors for power and precision. I believe it can also help you."

I had a very dramatic introduction to Davyn's power on a 320-yard par-4 playing directly into a brisk wind. I hit a driver some eighty yards short of the green. Davyn promptly took out his 3 iron and launched his ball into the stratosphere. While one playing companion cried "Call Houston," we watched the ball disappear over the horizon. When we reached the

green, we found the ball in the back bunker, a small meteorite's crater alongside marking its point of impact.

While I was impressed with Davyn's power, as we played more holes it became painfully apparent that accuracy was not his strongest suit. I recommended Davyn try the following drill to help him discover a smoother rhythm and greater balance . . . and exercise greater control of his ball's destination.

As shown in the photo sequence starting on page 101, "Step and Swing" for continuous repetitions of 30 seconds. Have a ball teed up, so you can immediately set up to a ball and make your swing with the same tempo.

Try this drill that has helped many players I coach achieve more fluidity and rhythm, two important elements of an effective golf swing. Watch for Davyn Nola, as this could be his year to win the World Long Drive Championship.

Davyn Nola of New Zealand regularly does exhibitions for corporate outings (www.golfdownunder.co.nz) and works with Golf Down Under Ltd., which specializes in golf tours to New Zealand. Known for its extraordinary natural beauty and abundant sheep population, New Zealand actually has more golf clubs per capita than any other country in the world!

6. MEDICINE BALL SWING: GAINING A COMPETITIVE EDGE

A golf swing involves 640 muscles—and practicing with a medicine ball helps train them to work in perfect harmony. Medicine ball training engages your bigger muscles while building muscle memory and strength through the entire range of your swing motion. I recognized the benefits of working with medicine balls early in my golf instruction career. When

Janet Crawford: "Since I understand the importance of developing athletic motion, working with a medicine ball is a key part of my training."

I introduced them, they drew the same looks as recommending yoga to a roomful of rugby players. They are now a staple of most training programs.

Golfers often ask me how much tension they should feel in different parts of their body during the swing. Swinging a medicine ball enables you to feel the right amount of muscular engagement and adopt a more athletic posture naturally. It also keeps you in shape when you can't make it out to the practice range.

With a medicine ball between your hands, take your golf posture and make your swing. This drill can also be used as a warm-up before you play golf. To build strength, use a slightly heavier ball working out in the gym.

JANET CRAWFORD, originally from San Francisco, California, is a novice golfer. As a former dancer, she looks forward to a long future with a graceful swing.

7. SMOOTH STARTING SWING: PRESHOT ROUTINE

Having a consistent preshot routine helps you execute your best swing with greater frequency. Setting up in the same position for swing after swing and going through the same procedure before you actually strike the ball are keys to peak performance.

Getting frozen over the ball at address for several seconds before beginning your swing is one common and counterproductive phenomenon that will likely make your backswing a jerky one. Although every swing breaks a state of inertia with a stretch of the arms (or a "heave," as David Lee contends), a little rhythmic motion preceding this will encourage a smoother, more fluid backswing.

As Jim Levine demonstrates below, you simply release the tension by a gentle waggle of the club with your arms and hands or a gentle rocking of the hips. Then set the club behind the ball and spend no more than an instant in place before beginning your swing.

Now you know why batters in baseball shift their weight continuously while waiting for the pitch, or tennis players rock in place while waiting to return a serve. Says Jim, "Standardizing everything I do has helped my game improve and be more consistent."

Jim Levine is a literary agent representing, among others, the author of this book. His easygoing personality hides an intense but cool competitor. He has shown his ability to play his best golf when the pressure is on—including a nine-hole meeting with the publishers. Jim, a lifelong 90s shooter, shot a one-over-par 37. Atria's Judith Curr expressed immediate interest in publishing the book.

8. WRIST ACTION

The term *Santellesque* may not have made it into your dictionary yet, but it is quickly working its way into every golf lexicographer's inventory. Named after the best-selling writer Chris Santella, it describes the wrists' failure to break, or "cock," in the correct vertical direction.

This failure results in a severe loss of clubhead speed and power, which makes even the most powerful and athletically gifted of individuals seem impotent.

The left photo of Chris on page 107 depicts a most rare case of absolutely "no cock" whatsoever, a dysfunction taken to the rarest state of perfection. When observing Chris swing for the first time, I couldn't help but wonder whether he wasn't having one over on me. I soon discovered this was in fact Chris's habitual swing motion. Ironically, the correct wrist action was actually familiar to Chris, a lifelong fisherman; he just had to apply it to his golf swing.

NO   YES

The old "little cock"—
Chris lacked power.

The new "big cock"—Chris
hits it long and straight.

Chris was not unaware of his problem. As he said, "I have taken lessons and received every conceivable advice. But Roberto's suggestion, which I think can work for you, didn't upset the flow of my swing with an abrupt 'setting of the wrists.' He advised that during the second half of the upswing, I simply allow the club to travel faster than everything else. This set my wrist automatically—and wow, what a sudden surge in power!"

The correct action of the wrists is to break in a vertical "up and down" manner/direction, as depicted on the following page.

Dr. Laurence Holt confirms in his seminal work *An Experimenter's Guide to the Full Golf Swing* that the final movement that causes the clubhead to attain its greatest acceleration involves release of the hands by means of a wrist movement (both wrists perform the same action)

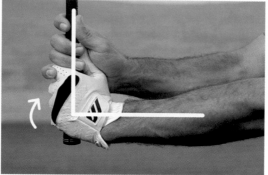

termed ulnar flexion. This combined motion is similar to the movement used to accelerate baseball bats, fishing rods, and other implements.

From his home state of Oregon, Chris continues to get more comfortable with his new move, pummeling the ball unfamiliar distances. Previously a 100s golfer, Chris has shot in the 80s several times and recently shot a 37! After the 9-hole score of his life, he picked up his ball and walked off the course. The consummate family man, Chris had rushed off to take his daughter to summer camp. . . . In the next edition of this book, Chris expects to be one of the "swing models." Until that time, enjoy these unusual photos of the Santella Evolution.

CHRIS SANTELLA is the author of the best-selling book *Fifty Places to Golf Before You Die.* He lives in Portland, Oregon, with his wife, Deidre, and two daughters, Annabel and Cassidy. A true renaissance man, Chris includes among his other hobbies fly-fishing, sailing, and bird-watching. Look for his titles on these beloved pastimes.

9. PUTTING ACCURACY

In the putting stroke, you will perform best by keeping your head and lower body completely still, no swaying or shifting. Any movement of your center of gravity will undermine the precision of your stroke. You can eliminate excess motion by practicing your stroke with your forehead placed against a wall.

"Roberto worked with me on my putting just before we embarked together on a trip to Spain," says Stan Robinson. "It was like the Ryder Cup every day. Roberto daily paired us with the host pros, and we won every match! This was largely due to my performance on the green. I putted lights out—including twelve one-putts on the challenging and quick greens of Valderrama! My short game has really improved, and I utilize this exercise to stay sharp."

As demonstrated below, Stan doesn't have to worry about keeping his head still, making a precision putting stroke with the help of Rivervale Country Club's snack shack.

As Stan demonstrates, it is a good idea to make a few strokes with your eyes closed to heighten your physical sensation of the correct movement, or should I say lack thereof.

To eliminate any excess lower body motion, just turn around and place your buttocks against the wall while you make your normal putting stroke. If this feels suddenly restrictive and different from your normal stroke, then you've likely been moving.

STAN ROBINSON is lead attorney for Robinson & Brog, a major law firm in New York City. One of his fondest golf memories includes a trip to Spain with the author, when Stan won nearly every match at Spain's premier clubs.

10. PITCHING AND CHIPPING PRECISION

Lateral motion undermines the precision of any player's shot game. Inside fifty yards of the green, your motion should be strictly rotational. You would be surprised, though, how prevalent a fault lateral motion is among amateurs. Even the most accomplished players I coach often need fine-tuning with this aspect of their game.

Belen Mozo finds this drill helpful to sharpen her skills around the green. As Belen demonstrates on the facing page, by adopting a stance that gives you a very narrow base, you are required to make a perfectly centered rotation. Any undesired lateral motion or shift in your center of gravity will cause you to lose your balance, which should be sufficient motivation to make you execute properly.

Belen comments, "When Roberto was living in Spain, he helped me in a similar way with my putting stroke, and I went on to win some important international junior titles. This exercise has a similar theme applied to approach shots around the green. It keeps you perfectly centered so that your angle of attack and generation of clubhead speed are consistent."

If you have had excessive movement in your strokes around the green, you should experience improvements almost immediately. This drill will help even the most advanced player to further refine their technique.

This exercise belongs in every golfer's developmental and practice repertory because it eliminates any precision-killing weight shift in your pitching motion.

BELEN DEMONSTRATES THREE STANCES

Stance 1: This is the easiest. Simply place a ball under your right heel when practicing around the greens. You will feel it when you shift.

Stance 2: Take your stance while pointing your right toe to the ground—you'll be immediately aware and, better yet, have no incentive to shift any weight to your right foot, as it will feel very uncomfortable.

Stance 3: Walking the Plank. Any lateral motion from such a stance will destabilize you, leading you to develop a pure rotation around a stable, fixed axis, and most important, pure accountability and accuracy.

11. EXCELLING IN SAND:
A DOLLAR GOES A LONG WAY

Figuring out how the sand wedge moves through the sand is crucial for good sand play. Experiment in a practice trap to learn what you'll need to do to get the clubhead moving. Practice with different textures—soft, fluffy sand and more hard-packed sand—to test how the clubhead passes through the sand when set square or open.

Here's one simple rule of thumb to facilitate a speedier discovery process: clubface open for fluffier sand and more square for firm sand.

This time-tested drill may seem almost too simple, but why not look for the easiest solutions to golf's complexities? This drill seems to work

well for everyone. As shown at left, place a dollar bill on top of the sand, with a little sand on the edge so it lies flat. The surface area of the bill represents the amount of sand you want to displace. Simply make your swing and take the dollar bill and the ball together to the hole.

"This drill is right on the money," says Joe Rassett, shown demonstrating it in the sequence above. "The drill really teaches you the dynamics of sand play without a lot of technical fanfare or explanation. If you have a tendency to get too steep or you are afraid to swing through the sand, this drill is your cure."

JOE RASSETT is a former PGA Tour player. He lives in Sarasota, Florida, and is the director of golf at the Longboat Key Club.

Part IV

Practice for Your Best Golf

11
YOUR COMPREHENSIVE PRACTICE PLAN

"Say, man, how do you get to Carnegie Hall?" "Practice, man, practice."
—DUKE ELLINGTON

THROUGH PRACTICE YOU DEVELOP a consistent technique that allows you to relax over the ball and swing without overthinking. A well-organized practice plan, however, requires some thought. How you best use your time will determine whether you are able to transform theory into reality.

This practice program is designed with that in mind. If you follow this regimen, in four months' time you will look back and realize how much progress you have made. It places your golf destiny in your hands.

Making your partner a "golf widow" is not an obligation—minimal but *regular* time need be committed to practice. Indeed, the Express Practice plan I've devised is an intense thirty- to forty-five-minute session formulated with your busy schedule in mind. For those who have the luxury of more time, I provide more extensive programs to match your ambitions.

I have designed three practice programs for you to choose from—the Express Practice, the 500 Club, and the Tour Pro. You can alter any program to meet your needs. Let these guidelines help you create structured and balanced sessions.

GETTING THE MOST OUT
OF YOUR PRACTICE SESSIONS

Priority 1: Design an Effective Program

An appropriately designed program should take into account your learning style and the time you have available for practice, as well as beginning with an honest assessment of your skill level. It must also consider your temperament and personality. Some individuals are capable of sustaining long periods of concentration; others work more effectively in short spurts. As my host and I walked the course at a private club in Connecticut, he pointed out the tennis star Ivan Lendl to me. Lendl was all alone, already immersed in a sea of white as he chipped balls to the practice green. When we made the turn some hours later, he was still there, his head down, steadfastly chipping away.

Priority 2: Practice with a Purpose

Many players dedicate sufficient time to practice, but lack a plan for improving their technique and overall golf game. A practice routine lacking a specific or overall strategy is time wasted. You should approach your session much as a pianist does a concert or an aspiring attorney the bar exam. Emulate the habits of great players who work on something specific during each session—their swing, setup, or rhythm—rather than just hitting balls. You too will be best served having a systematic approach with a specific outcome in mind.

Priority 3: Choose Quality over Quantity

Individuals delude themselves by thinking that they will achieve excellence at the game simply from the intensity of their passion for it. I emphasize channeling that energy appropriately and putting craft over enthusiasm. Practice smarter, not harder.

Priority 4: Avoid Injury

Unless you just stepped out of your yoga or Pilates class, always warm up with some stretches and some no-stress pitch shots. Even better, take a short walk or engage in a few minutes of light aerobic activity before taxing your body. Also, always aim to achieve perfect motion. Injuries most often occur when you get careless with technique and preparation.

Priority 5: Commit to the Cause

Focused time is a necessary ingredient for perfecting any craft. If your schedule allows, start by blocking out a specific amount of time per day or week for practice time. If you have a tournament on Saturday, it is better to practice a little bit each day than to cram on Friday and expect success.

Priority 6: Integrate Practice Drill and "Real Swing"

Reduce the time lapse between drill and normal execution so that your body memory is fresh. If you are working on your shoulder turn with the prescribed drill in this book, for example, don't do it for ten minutes and then rest. Instead, execute the drill, and then immediately execute your normal swing.

Priority 7: Use Creative Performance Benchmarks

To close a practice session, put your skills to the test. For example, take ten balls and see how many you can put inside one club length of the hole from ten, twenty, and thirty yards away. Do this as a regular way to monitor your progress.

THREE SAMPLE PRACTICE PLANS

The Express Practice (30–45 minutes)

The Express Practice Plan, besides being a short, well-rounded practice session, is a great preround warm-up. It will take you from thirty to forty-five minutes.

Not everyone has the luxury of time enjoyed by my uncle Jim Tivnan, who went from a twelve to a two handicap when he changed jobs and became a schoolteacher. Not everyone has summers off, but if you plan your practice intelligently, you can make extraordinary gains. The Express program has your busy schedule in mind. It is long enough to have a real effect, but short enough to maintain your absolute focus.

What craftsman, grown old in his trade, has not asked himself with a sudden qualm whether he has spent his time wisely?
—UNKNOWN

As a warm-up, it gets you ready for play. When you use it as a daily practice session, you can vary the program, doing the parts that best target your problem areas. You may wonder how I finish all these exercises and shots in thirty minutes. The workout's arranged so that there's little need for resting in between.

A great warm-up is key to bringing out your best performance. Just as an orchestra tunes up before a performance, you need to tune instrument and technique. Movement Preparation, a full stretching program, is step 1, and will serve you well as a prelude to your fitness workout. Game Preparation, getting your swing and strokes ready, is step 2. In short, you will soon learn the value of preparation.

Movement Preparation

Here are a few prioritized stretches, a "quick" stretch version. However, do them slowly. This should not replace the full stretching program and workout found in chapter 12.

Roll Down

Lateral Oblique Stretch

Pectoralis Minor and Major Stretch

Speed Skater Rotation

Game Preparation

The point of using this program as your warm-up is to do a little of every-thing before you actually begin play. Pregame is not the time to attempt an overhaul of your technique. If you begin with putting or pitching, you get the flow of gravity going in your body, and that rhythm will be more likely to carry over into your full swing.

- 20 pitches (10 each from fairway and rough, in sets of increasing distance—i.e., 10, 20, 30, 40, and 50 yards) with your sand or pitch-ing wedge. Unless you are preparing for a round on a links course or it's very windy, stay with these lofted clubs. You can practice less lofted swings in your more extensive practice session.

- 40 full swings—10 each with short, middle, and long irons and driver.

- 20 chips with your sand or pitch wedge and one less lofted club, such as an 8 iron (5 ball reps from four positions: uphill, downhill, right side, left side).

- 10 sand shots. If the course does not have a practice bunker, then look for some deep rough and practice your technique to get the feel of swinging through resistance.

- 30 putts. Begin by placing five balls at the side of the green. Hit each ball farther than the last until you finally reach the opposite side; repeat the exercise from another spot. Then, as shown in the left photo above, place five balls in a straight line and putt them to the hole; repeat on a different line. Finally, as shown at right, place a spare club on the green parallel to your target line, and putt five balls from three feet and five balls from four feet.

The 500 Club (1.5–2 hours): Developing and Perfecting Your Craft

- 10 minutes of stretching, balance, and coordination exercises from the fitness section

- 100 full swings—drives and fairway woods (30 minutes)

- 200 pitches, chips, and sand shots (30 minutes)

- 100 putts (30 minutes)

The Tour Pro: The 500 Club Plus an All-Golf Training Day

For the overachievers who can dedicate an entire day to their passion, this is a perfect day's golf training. Do not attempt this unless you are in good shape. Consult your doctor if this is more exercise than you would perform normally.

- 100 full swings—drives and fairway woods

- 200 pitches, chips, and sand shots

- 100 putts

- 18 holes of golf

- 1 hour in the gym—exercise and motion study

- 1 hour of studying swing images

Sample Schedule

8 am: Wakeup call—shower, dress, breakfast

9:30–10: Aerobic warm-up and stretching

10–11: Short-game practice

11–12: Full-swing practice

12–2 pm: Lunch and rest

2–2:30: Warm-up

2:30–6:30: 18 holes of golf

6:30–7:15: Fitness workout

8 pm: Dinner

10 pm: Video study and review

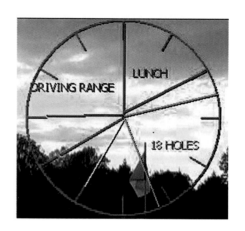

. . . Oh, and yes, after a day like this take two aspirin and soak in a hot Jacuzzi.

WORKING IN TANDEM

Practice can be a solitary act that allows you to work things out for yourself, building your confidence and providing a true sense of accomplishment. But you might not always want to practice alone, and might find greater enjoyment and challenge practicing with someone else.

Partnering with a friend, relative, or regular playing companion can be an extremely productive way to train. Support and shared enthusiasm can result in mutual encouragement and inspiration. Nearly every facet of the game can be practiced in tandem. As shown on pages 127 and 128, you can discover interesting and rewarding ways to train with a partner. I often "play catch," pitching the ball back and forth with players I coach. Here Belen Mozo and I demonstrate some fun and productive collaborations. You can do this too.

MEDICINE BALL THROWS

Besides being a great workout, medicine ball throws allow you the freedom to work on your form without concern for ball and target.

CHIP AND PITCH FOR TWO

Chipping and pitching back and forth is great practice and makes the time go by faster and more productively when there's a long wait on a tee. Move around to vary the distance and the type of lie.

CENTERING YOUR SHORT GAME

Keeping the axis perfectly still and centered is a key for precision.

PRACTICING WITH A NET

Many people shudder at the idea of a practice net, preferring to watch a ball fly, even if it slices forty yards, diagonally crossing from one corner of the range to the other. They would do well to discover the merits of working on just the basic mechanics of the swing and ball contact.

There is no better place to do this than the comfort of your home. I am a great believer in using a hitting net or some other mechanism that allows you to focus on your swing rather than the flight of the ball. Having a net set up in your garage or backyard lets you do this. It's particularly useful when you are learning something new or making a change to your swing.

I have worked with golfers using a net over the winter months to spectacular effect. Whatever downside there is to not seeing ball flight is greatly outweighed by the benefits. In any case, you will make your visits to a traditional driving range anyway.

Before leaving for his office, David Nolan makes a few swings in the courtyard of his New York City town house.

This medium allows you to work on the swinging motion in a wonderfully focused way. At Jim McLean's Golf School at Doral, for example, there are retractable nets in the main hitting bays. If you were to ask the instructors why, they would probably answer, "Effectiveness."

One extreme example of practice net devotion was Cathy Whitworth, one of the game's great players, whose coach made her hit balls into a net for the first six months of learning before allowing her to step onto a golf course. I wish I could shake that man's hand. Fred Couples is another current player who used a net effectively in the off-season and the formative stages of his game.

Developing a good technique is your objective. It is counterproductive to watch inconsistent ball flight and results. A net *focuses your attention on process rather than results.* It also gives you that competitive advantage over your companions whose clubs have gone into hibernation.

Besides the net, a hitting surface is necessary. Few mats offer the feel and real hitting action of the Softee Mat, the closest thing to hitting off actual "grass." It provides a more authentic divot-taking feel with your iron shot, with little of the bouncing and jarring of your usual driving-range mats, which often fatigue and can even injure your wrists.

In the course of an afternoon you can set up your own at-home driving range. I recommend it highly.

12
GOLF FITNESS TRAINING

FITNESS TRAINING PROGRAMS positively influence your performance. Your physical well-being is a determining factor in how powerful and efficient your swing motion is likely to be. Of course, this assumes mastery of proper swing mechanics, but since you have read this far, your technique is nearly perfect, right? We can now focus on the main actor in the swing equation—your body.

Today, the best players combine talent with bodies fine-tuned to a level that is consistent with most other professional athletes. Almost every tour pro has a regular workout routine and a trainer. Finally, the body has received its deserved appreciation in the golf world.

You might ask yourself, "Why should I start stretching and lifting weights when I'm not a tour pro?" The short answer is plain and simple— better performance. Whatever your skill level, the appropriate conditioning program is going to help you get the most out of your golf swing.

A good fitness program will allow you to fully exploit your base/ existing capability. Many exercises in this program focus on core training. With a strong core, it's amazing how much power and force you can generate. It's a strong base to build on, and creates much more ability and freedom to move. Several exercises enforce corrective motion and

Good luck keeping up with my eighty-four-year-old uncle and role model, Jim Tivnan.

muscle memory to refine your technique. Other exercises will focus on your body's alignment, in order to exploit your flexibility and balance potential. You need not be limited by your body and make it a scapegoat for your not achieving your goals. Being in shape will be better for you, period.

TRAINING PROGRAM:
GAIN THAT COMPETITIVE ADVANTAGE

"You're trying to kill me," said Zola Gold, one of my senior students, after I outlined a fitness training program he would soon begin. My intentions were quite the contrary. Besides its general health benefits, the training regimen I proposed would help him build a stronger swing. Sure enough, after a challenging first session, three weeks later he said he was feeling better and stronger than he had in years.

Admittedly, there's a degree of discomfort associated with challenging yourself physically, but as Mark Verstegen, recognized as one of the world's sports performance experts and author of *Core Performance,* has stated: "I prefer to look at it as a metaphor for life. You need to get out of your comfort zone, avoid complacency, and try new things to grow and progress. As in life, it's important to remember that this discomfort and pain will pass."

Committing a limited amount of time to a golf-specific training program develops the following:

- Strength

- Coordination

- Flexibility

- Balance

- Endurance

The exercises throughout this book develop your capacity in each of these areas. As a golfer, you do not need the extreme muscular strength of a weight lifter or the maximum endurance of a marathon runner. But you will be well served if you achieve a little of both.

Before you begin, here are some answers to some concerns and questions you may have:

How will a golf fitness program affect my swing? Many people are concerned that lifting weights will make them muscle-bound, thus compromising their flexibility. This is a huge misconception. Although adding a significant muscle mass to your frame could initially affect your golf swing unpredictably, a balanced fitness program that includes weight lifting will increase your strength, coordination, and flexibility. If you do more repetitions and less weight, you will be working toward gaining lean muscle mass that is capable of endurance-based activity, as golf requires.

All elements of conditioning—alignment, balance, flexibility, strength, and cardiorespiratory endurance—are interrelated. A change in one affects all the others. It is an evolutionary process, so you will incorporate this increase in strength and mobility in time.

The most strategically sound program interweaves regular golf practice sessions with workouts so that your swing progresses smoothly with your body. Just hitting balls into a net will allow your body to adjust to its changing physicality so that your golf game has a chance to keep pace. Otherwise, like an adolescent after a growth spurt, expect to awake to a new and unfamiliar body.

How long and frequent should my workouts be? Ideally, you should incorporate your workout as part of your daily regimen, dedicating between forty-five minutes and one hour.

If your workout is your first activity of the day, I recommend a hot shower and/or a few minutes of light, easy cardio—e.g., a brisk walk, bicycle, or elliptical machine. Then proceed to the first group of stretches and coordination exercises, which will get your muscles optimally lengthened. This is a perfect prelude to playing golf or lifting weights.

DETERMINING YOUR GOALS

To improve your overall fitness, organize a program that balances strength, flexibility, and aerobic activities. Your objectives in training can be modest or ambitious. You decide the intensity and length of your training sessions.

- If you are just beginning, easing into a conditioning routine will save you time and aggravation because you are less likely to injure yourself by asking your body to do something it is not yet prepared to do. Listen to your body; if an exercise feels wrong or painful, don't do it.

- If you are in good shape already, you might want to take the opportunity to discover new ways to improve your performance mobility and get into the best shape of your life.

All training should be done with presence of mind and body to create an inspiring performer who can master all the steps efficiently and with ease.

—MIKHAIL BARYSHNIKOV

Some good guidelines to follow:

- **Work efficiently.** The exercise program that follows is arranged so that there is little need for rest in between exercises. You can get more done in less time.

- **Train for performance.** One idea universally agreed upon by kinesiologists and physical therapists is to train for the specific movement/range of motion required by a sport—that is to say, to use relevant exercises. The medicine ball exercises are popular for that very reason. They strengthen muscles, while adequately training the body for the exact physical requirements of the swing. Furthermore, they allow you to focus on your swing technique without the distraction of ball and target. Training the right muscle groups and range of motion will encourage a new, more efficient and powerful swing motion. If your range of motion is limited, don't worry. Exercises in this program are well structured and engage your muscles in balanced movements that apply specifically to golf.

- **Think of your strength training as part of golf training.** You will note that several of the exercises are performed as forms of the golf swing.

- **Be a perfectionist.** Strive for perfect motion and form when doing exercises. Lackadaisical technique can result in injury. Rather than going about the process like a robot, take the time to pause and reflect on the procedure, the experience, and your progress.

Vanities aside, love your mirror. You can ensure proper form by developing a good relationship with the mirror. All weight and movement training exercises are well served by monitoring your motions to make sure you maintain proper form.

Begin Your Workout with Five Minutes of Aerobic Activity and Stretching

Rather than try to stretch as you play, or during the course of your round, your goal should be to *be prepared* on the first tee. Five minutes of brisk walking or calisthenics is the perfect prelude to any stretching because it gets your blood circulating. Getting the blood to your muscles before any focused, muscle-isolating exercises is of the utmost importance. Whether you are going to the first tee or the gym, a few stretches will ensure that you are physically ready before any strenuous lifting or swinging. To be effective, stretches should be ideally held for twenty to thirty seconds. And be sure to keep breathing. Don't hold your breath!

Erin Johnson is a highly respected health fitness professional living in New York City. She is certified as a medical exercise specialist, a health fitness instructor through the American College of Sports Medicine, and a Pilates mat instructor. After captaining the Minnesota Vikings cheerleaders, she began her career as an exercise specialist in physical therapy at the Beth Israel Medical Center. Erin is currently the founder and director of postrehabilitation at Beth Israel.

Erin was a major influence on my fitness training, so I thought it only appropriate that she take you through many of the exercises that have had positive results for me. Without any further ado, turn the page and let Erin lead you through your program.

1. Roll Over

Objective: Flexibility

Start standing straight, with legs together. Slowly let your head fall forward and continue rolling down. Think vertebra by vertebra. Let your body hang while keeping your abdominals engaged. Legs should be straight but not locked.

A variation: While you are already there, bend your knees and straighten them for a great stretch of your hamstrings. To deepen the stretch, shift the weight forward, more toward your toes than your heels.

2. Sideways Stretch

Objective: Flexibility

Start by standing with feet wider than hip-width apart. Bend to the right and slide your hand down the side of your right leg while the other arm goes up and over to the same side. Keep your shoulders down when your arm is up. You should feel the stretch along the opposite side of the body.

3. Pectoral Stretch

Objective: Flexibility

Stand with feet together. Clasp hands together behind your back. Bring your arms up and over as you bend forward.

4. Speed Skater

Objective: Flexibility and Range of Motion

Keep weight even between both sides to start. Bring one arm to the opposite leg and slightly bend the knees. The other arm rotates and extends up to the back. You should feel the stretch through the torso and the shoulder of the extended arm.

5. Lower Back Stretch and Lengthening

Objective: Flexibility and Range of Motion

Stand with feet wider than hip-width apart. Bring both arms down to one side. Then rotate the arm opposite the leg you are leaning toward, and stretch it straight up to the ceiling. Turn your focus to the hand extended up.

6. Hip Hinge

Objective: Balance and Alignment

To prepare, extend one leg back with the toe on the floor. Make sure to keep the hips even and facing directly forward. Slowly start to lift the leg behind you. The upper body should move forward as the leg is going up, to counterbalance your body weight. Bring the leg up only as far as you can without arching your back. Hold 2 to 5 seconds and begin to come back to center by contracting the glutes and hamstrings of the standing leg.

7. Planks

Objective: Core Stability and Strength

Start on your stomach and pull up to your elbows and the balls of the feet. Make sure your shoulders are directly above your elbows. The back is neutral—no arching! Keep your legs together and straight. Contract your abdominals to maintain this position. Think of lengthening the body, but keep stable and hold. Hold only as long as you can without changing the proper body position.

A variation: Start on your hands and knees, your hips directly above your knees and your shoulders directly above your elbows. Keep your spine neutral while extending the opposite arm and leg. Keep hips even and spine straight.

8. Side Plank

Objective: Core Stability, Alignment, and Strength

Same idea as the former exercise, except that you brace yourself on your elbow and forearm while maintaining the integrity of your spinal column. You may feel confident after some practice to add the more difficult version on the right.

9. Lower Twist

Objective: Core Stability and Abdominal Strength

Lie on your back with your arms out to the sides and knees up and bent at 90 degrees. Start to rotate legs together to one side. Deepen your abdominals to control your movement and to bring the legs back to center and over to the other side. Keep your shoulders pressed against the floor.

10. Marching Crunch

Objective: Core Stability and Abdominal Strength

Lie with knees bent and back flat to the ground. Put your hands behind your head, elbows wide. Contract your upper body up to the tips of the shoulder blades. Hold that upper-body position for the duration of the exercise. While lowering the opposite leg, bring one knee toward the chest until the knee is directly above the hip; focus on using the abs to do this. Then alternate to the other side.

11. Seated Rotation with Medicine Ball

Objective: Core Stability and Strength

Sit with legs straight in front of you and together. Keep your back straight and abdominals contracted to maintain neutral spine. Hold a weighted medicine ball with both hands, arms extended straight out and parallel with your legs. Rotate the torso, using your abs, to one side and then back to center. Repeat to the other side. Do only as many reps as you can while maintaining proper form.

12. Lunge with a Medicine Ball Twist

Objective: Core and Lower Body Stability

In addition to increasing strength and range of motion, this is an ideal exercise for building the important torso-hip separation that is necessary for creating torque. The exercise also develops lower body stability, because it requires you to naturally brace and resist with your lower body.

Start from a standing position, holding a medicine ball with your arms extended in front of you. Take a big step forward with your right foot and turn your torso in the same direction. Return to your starting position and step forward on your left foot, rotating in the same direction.

13. Rear Deltoid Flys

Objective: Strength

Stand with feet together or hip-width apart, holding a weight in each hand. Bend forward 45 degrees, keeping your back straight and abs pulled in. Start with arms down, palms facing each other and elbows slightly bent. Open the arms to the sides, using the shoulders and back. Always controlling the movement of the weights, exhale on the movement up and inhale on the way down.

14. Frontal Deltoid Flys

Objective: Strength (10–12 repetitions)

Stand straight with your feet shoulder-width apart, your knees slightly bent, one foot forward and the other back. Slowly raise your arms in front of you to shoulder height. Don't rock your hips or swing your arms for momentum. Hold for a second, and then slowly return to the starting position.

15. Pull-Downs

Objective: Latissimus Dorsi Strength

16. Weighted Swing

Objective: Strength and Range of Motion and Technique

Make swings with a five- or ten-pound weight plate either in your gym or at home. This exercise helps build a powerful swing and trains the necessary and natural rotation of the forearms/hands/clubface along the arc. In the second frame, notice how my thumbs are pointing to the ceiling, the plate perfectly vertical—with the golf club this would translate into the toe of the clubface pointing skyward. The extra weight will engage your entire core and help you achieve pure rotation along the natural arc. It will also help any player who has a tendency to break the wrists laterally on the takeaway. To double the effectiveness of this exercise, keep a club nearby and make a few swings immediately.

17. Double-Ball Exercise

Objective: Balance and Lower Body Strength and Stability

There is a fair chance you have seen this exercise in print or on the Golf Channel. Get balanced on the ball and make your golf swing. On your first attempt you will find this exercise quite challenging. Do not be discouraged; over time you will find it easier to maintain your balance while swinging. You can begin with a putting stroke or a half-swing until you find your equilibrium.

18. Arc Symmetry and Extension

Objective: Technique Development

Former touring pro Donna White loves this exercise for arc symmetry, which keeps you from "breaking down" throughout your stroke. The object is to maintain the tension in the bands while you make your putting, chipping, or pitching motion.

SHORT GAME

| *Yes* | *Yes* | *No* |

19. Full Swing Extension

Objective: Extension through the "Hitting Area"

Make full swings with the bands. Make sure that you maintain the same tension in the bands and that your arms are comfortably extended when your hands are at waist height.

13
VIDEO SWING ANALYSIS

THE DIGITAL ERA IS RESHAPING everything we do. Both golfer and instructor today have extraordinary resources in technology and information. Turn on the Golf Channel any evening, and you will be quickly up-to-date on the latest techniques and theories of the game's top teachers and thinkers.

Video swing analysis is a significant element of this technological revolution, and I have always been a strong proponent of it as a complement to an effective training program. It allows a level of empiricism and certainty that verbal critique can never achieve, letting you view the general motion of your swing, as well as delve into the more nuanced elements of swing plane, swing tempo, posture angles, impact position, and so on. Video swing analysis is readily available to the consumer, with some software versions costing about the same as a golf lesson!

The utility of this great resource depends on the user, however. If you have absorbed the lessons given in the previous chapters, your knowledge of technique may make you an able diagnostician. Nonetheless, while continuing your usual course of lessons from your local pro, you can monitor your swing's progress. The objective is to empower yourself. Seeing yourself swing the first time may come as a shock, but it gives you a true depiction of reality. You would not be the first athlete to think you are doing one thing when you are actually doing something else.

VIDEOTAPING YOUR SWING

With swing-analysis technology, every movement can be caught in a freeze frame.

Setting up your own video studio is easy!

Having read the previous twelve chapters, you now know what good form looks like. Consider setting up your own "studio" to analyze your swing and that of your friends. While this might seem an ambitious undertaking, once you have the camera and software, you can learn the whole process in about an hour.

PURCHASING A VIDEO CAMERA

How do I choose a video camera? Don't waste your time worrying about this. Nearly any video camera on the market today will suffice to capture your swing. An expensive video camera with high resolution, still pictures, and the best audio quality is nice, but not necessary. The following two features are important:

- *Sports mode function* or manual shutter control allows you to set the camera at a fast enough shutter speed to catch the fast motion of the swing without blurring. Most cameras have a sports mode function, but not all have a fast enough shutter speed. If you are buying in a large electronics store, you can test it out right there. Have the salesman tape your swing or make a super-fast motion with your hand or arm, and then view it frame-by-frame. The more clearly you can see your hand, the better.

- *Large LCD screen.* While almost all cameras have an LCD screen, not all are large enough to provide a worthy viewing experience. Since you will want to have a look at your swing on the practice range or golf course and may not have your laptop in tow, the larger the LCD screen, the better. Some models offer a three-and-a-half- or four-inch LCD screen.

SOFTWARE

There are several software programs that can provide you with adequate tools for analyzing your swing. I use V1 Professional because it offers a wide variety of functions. Fortunately, they make an affordable version for the consumer (approximately $100), as well as a professional version for instructors. All the software packages allow you to capture, replay, and draw. V1 has the most functionality, in my opinion, and excellent tech service—important when you have questions or problems.

FILMING

- **Hold the camera still.** The camera should be perfectly still when you're filming. If you don't have a tripod handy, you can substitute your driver, bracing your elbow on the grip end of the golf club so that the camera remains relatively still.

- **Choose your point of view.** Film either from behind (referred to as "down the line") or facing the golfer (referred to as "face on"). When filming down the line, position the camera in between the line of the feet and ball at about torso height. When facing the golfer, simply center the player in the middle of the frame.

- **Film as closely as possible for maximum resolution.** There is no need to include much foreground in the frame. Feet should be precisely at the bottom of the frame. A camera with a wider lens angle will allow you to get closer. If your "studio" occupies a small space, you may want to purchase a separate wide-angle lens. After filming each swing, voice the shot's outcome, e.g., "way right" or "on target." This provides useful information for your later analysis, since you are not likely to remember the details of each swing.

REVIEWING VIDEO

- Have a look at your swing in slow motion before making any closer analysis.

- Be a disciplined self-coach; focus on one thing at a time.

If your software program allows, trim the video clips once you have downloaded them to your computer, so that each one begins with the first motion of your upswing and ends at your finish. The clips should be less than 2 seconds and "weigh" about 2 MB. Video files are memory-heavy, so you may want to store your clips on a CD to keep your computer running efficiently.

ACKNOWLEDGMENTS

Failure is an orphan, but success has many fathers.

—NAPOLEON

THIS BOOK WAS NOT BORN from a sole mother hen. During the summer of 2006, Jean Borgatti, Nick Simonds, Eric Levin, Christian Bandler, and my literary agent, Jim Levine, were with me at critical stages, and gave generously of themselves. I am thankful for their sound judgment and persistent encouragement.

I also thank the instructors and students with whom I have had the opportunity to work. My development has benefited from dialogue with several professional colleagues: the encouragement of David Leadbetter, the fine intellect of Michael Hebron, conversations with David Lee and Jim McClean, and the brilliant research and writings of Dr. Laurence Holt.

World travel has also opened my mind to a great many perspectives. I lived in Europe for seven years and had the pleasure of coaching in virtually all of the golf meccas of England, Ireland, Spain, Portugal, and Scotland. Unexpected treasures include experiences instructing golf in Australia, Brazil, China, Cuba, England, and Australia. I am grateful that my second teaching assignment was in the ultracompetitive environment of the City of New York, home of many of the world's top golf clubs. I was continually pushed to develop the most effective system to help golfers achieve excellence. In Seville, Spain, where I worked with the 2004 World Golf Championships, I was fortunate to be a welcomed professional at the Royal Club of Seville, ranked among Europe's top courses.

I must thank Gary Palis and his team at Interactive Frontiers, whose powerful video swing-analysis program, V1 Professional, allows me and others to offer a superior service to players we coach.

Thanks to my extraordinary literary agent, Jim Levine, for accepting an additional editorial role for some golf tuition. To Nicolas Haro, Hugo Arturi, and Henry Hargreaves for their photography work. The fitness section was augmented by Mark Vergested, Erin Johnson, Guy LaFebre, and Lauren Yalango. Many thanks also to my literary support group, especially Andrew Arkin and Ron Vioni, who carefully read drafts and offered valuable suggestions. Other contributors include Tanya Koslovska, Uday Mahtani, Janet Crawford, Al Raymond, JoAnn Seltun, Patrick Lencioni, Joel Fedder, Ellen Fedder, Richard Goldwater, Julia Szanton, Rick La Pointe, Carol Fazzio, and Avron Brog.

I would like to extend a special thanks to Michael Welly, general manager of the Longboat Key Club, for his belief in and support for this project. I spend the winter months at this beautiful golf resort and spa on Florida's Gulf Coast as a featured guest instructor. Many of the scenic pictures were taken on location.

On the European front, the splendid golf club of Quinta da Ria, Portugal, which runs along a pristine and environmentally protected Atlantic coastline, was the beautiful setting for photos in Parts I and II. Another location was Rivervale Country Club, a Donald Ross–designed gem, just a short drive from New York City.

Finally, many thanks to my publishers at Atria, especially Nick Simonds and Judith Curr, for their unwavering commitment to this project.